Acknowledgments

We would like to acknowledge the following people for volunteering their time and effort in creating this anthology:

Lawson Inada for inspiring us.

Byron Wong, former president of the Thymos organization, for bringing people together to initiate this project.

Members of the Thymos organization, including Victor Lam, Hoang Nguyen, Jenny Lee, Monica Sack, David Kong, Liani Reeves, Bao-loc Nguyen, and Curtis Choy.

Doug Katagiri for designing the anthology cover and interior pages.

Patti Sakurai, Patti Duncan, Lawson Inada, and Ed Lin for facilitating the writing workshops.

Sunny Woan from *Kartika Review*, James Chan from the Alpha Asian blog, and Michelle Ing of Crowell-Ing for their guidance on the publishing process.

Frank Chin and Curtis Choy, who were our guests for the original event that inspired this work.

Our Gold Sponsors for the event with Lawson Inada: Crowell-Ing, Oregon Heath and Science University, Diverse and Empowered Employees of Portland, Janet and John Jay, the Oregon Commission on Asian Affairs, the Korean American Citizens League, and the Center for Diversity and Multicultural Affairs.

The Red and Black Café, Aaron Adams and Dinae Horne of Portobello Vegan Trattoria, and Jeremy Adams and Andrea Pastor of Cellar Door Coffee Roasters for their generous contributions to our events and fundraisers.

Everyone who helped coordinate, donated to, participated

in and publicized the writing workshops and all other events associated with this anthology.

All the authors who submitted their writing to us for consideration. We appreciate everyone who let us read their work. Thanks in particular to the authors who gave us their generous permission to include their pieces in our anthology. Our project would not have been possible without them.

We would like to dedicate this anthology
to all Asian American activist writers and artists.
Keep writing and creating!

Contents

The Asian American activist organization Thymos owes deep gratitude to former Oregon Poet Laureate Lawson Inada for coming up with the idea for this anthology. On July 22, 2008, Thymos invited Lawson to be a guest lecturer for one of our events at the Red and Black Café in Portland, Oregon. Lawson began the discussion about activism by asking us to draw a map of the various places we had lived. He went around the room, and we told him where we had been and how our paths had finally brought us to the Red and Black. It was a fascinating journey as we all learned about one another's lives and backgrounds, and we saw exactly how complex and nuanced we all are. It was Lawson who provided the initial inspiration for this project, and we are grateful for his contribution.

Introduction
Asian American Activism in the Twenty-first Century

What does it mean to be an Asian American in the twenty-first century?

In the mainstream American perspective, clichéd stereotypes about Asian people as model minorities, asexual techno-geeks, hypersexual dragon ladies, perpetual foreigners, or Yellow Peril "threats" continue to persist—though they are frequently concealed behind politically correct slogans like colorblindness and diversity.

One obstacle that Asian Americans thus face is the inability to claim an identity and culture that are defined by the Asian American community itself, rather than how mainstream society defines us. Whether it's dealing with popular stereotypes or the effects of institutional racism, many problems confronting Asian Americans ultimately stem from a lack of power. This includes the power to express our lives, histories, and beliefs in a manner that is true to our lived experiences. And in an era where the mass media exerts pervasive influence to shape the very nature of Asian America for ourselves and others, this is more important than ever.

Our book's title, *Where Are You From?: An Anthology of Asian American Writing*, echoes the common prejudice expressed by the majority culture that Asian Americans do not belong or "fit" in America. Some people have trouble believing that Asian faces can also be American. Being asked where we come from is both frustrating and irritating to Asian Americans whose families deserve to be credited with having lived in this country for many generations, helping to build it through their contributions as merchants, soldiers, teachers, salespeople, doctors, lawyers, politicians, fathers, mothers, and children—roles that other non-Asian Americans fill throughout their lives. We were instrumental in Hawaii's sugar industry. We were significant in the building of the transcontinental railroad that eventually helped America become economically powerful. We have been in the United States for a long time. But because we are still being asked where we come from, we are sharing our various answers through this book. We hope people will understand us better and help us fight the racism, prejudice, and discrimination that still exist. This anthology will also serve as a historical record of who we are at the beginning of the twenty-first century.

The writings in this book recognize that Asian Americans live complex lives. Before the civil rights era, Asian Americans endured mass racial riots, internment, and other forms of violence that were obvious and less easy to deny. Racism against Asian Americans in our current times is occasionally "soft" to the point that it's hard to define as "racism," a term that connotes violence, outward prejudice, and hatred. Instead of violence and open hatred, Asian Americans sometimes deal with more subtle forms of discrimination in terms of cultural stereotyping, social marginalization, and racial "Othering." This kinder, gentler version of the persistent anti-Asian sentiment found throughout American history distorts perceptions of Asian people today and is one of our most potent enemies. Racism and racial violence most certainly exist in our modern times as exemplified by the killing of Vincent Chin or the racialized sexual targeting of Asian women; it's clear that physical forms of violence and racism are still occurring. Yet internalized racial beliefs, rather than the cruder, open forms of racism, are harder to combat because they are "hidden." Their effects are far-reaching because they affect Asian Americans at every level of their daily lives, including jobs we are considered for (we have yet to elect an Asian American President of the United States); how much we are paid; and how high we can aspire (e.g., the bamboo ceiling). Asian American activism must seek to counteract both visible and invisible forms of racism against our group as well as other minority groups.

The greatest psychological barrier to overcoming this benevolent form of internalized racism comes in the form of the "model minority" myth. In the 1960s, journalist William Peterson coined the term "model minority" to describe how Japanese American cultural mores helped Japanese Americans to succeed in the U.S.[1] This concept was based upon a comparison between those races who have succeeded and those who have not. Asian Americans are the "good" minorities who work and are financially stable, stay away from crime, and live almost like the white majority—unlike the "bad" minorities such as African and Latino Americans who just make lots of noise. The most common argument employed by believers of the Asian model minority idea is to cite the socio-economic success of some Asian Americans as representative of the entire community: "Look at how *you people* attend such great schools. Look at how the crime rates and poverty levels among *you people* are so low. What are you complaining about?"

While the model minority myth sounds complimentary on the surface, the effect of believing in such a myth creates an atmosphere in which Asian Americans cease to invest time and energy in self-reflection. We begin to think of ourselves as having "already made it," and we stop improving ourselves, believing that we've already crossed the finish line while the race is still afoot. We know that we have yet to achieve parity with the majority culture because we see our lack of representation in the media, corporate boardrooms, and politics—yet we allow ourselves to fall into complacency. Equally problematic is the perception of Asian Americans by non-Asian Americans. Non-Asians, too, fall into the bad habit of internalizing beliefs without challenging them or taking a closer look at reality, and they cease to recognize our situation for what it is.

The typical activist reaction to the model minority myth is to challenge the findings. For example, one can argue that median household incomes among Asian Americans are higher because there are typically more wage earners living under one roof. Or if data is sorted differently, not all immigrant communities (especially certain groups within the Southeast Asian refugee diaspora) are financially successful. These are legitimate arguments, but our activist approach to the model minority myth is motivated by the desire to take readers of our anthology beyond seeing Asian Americans through the lens of money or scholastic achievements. As trite as it may sound, Asian Americans are people. We want to be seen for who we are deep down inside and not judged just by how we look or the statistics and stereotypes of our group.

One important battle for Asian American cultural activists is to create our own images and to fight for recognition of these self-created images from mainstream America; we don't have to accept identities thrust upon us by the majority culture. It is a sad fact that Asian American women between the ages of fifteen and twenty-four have the highest suicide rates of any ethnicity. It is telling that Asian American males have fallen into a depressing cycle of violence, but our activism should not be a defensive maneuver lest we condemn ourselves to self-definition through the very mainstream prejudice we seek to overcome. Instead, we need to envision Asian American identity, culture, and politics on our own terms, through our own experiences and perspectives. These efforts will yield the greatest results if we share the truth of our lived realities. In the words of Lawson Inada, we want to tell people where we come from ... where we're *really* from.

Byron Wong
Larry Yu
Valerie Katagiri
Portland, 2012

NOTES

[1]Andrew Chin, "A Brief History of the 'Model Minority' Stereotype." *Modelminority.com*. N.p., 4 April 2001. Web. 13 Nov. 2011.

Eating Noodles
by Lawson Inada

Even though it is cold outside,
the windows of the noodle shop
are covered with humid warmth
as columns of fragrant steam
arise from bowls of broth.

The crowd, of course, is busy—
children, adults, the very elderly
eating, conversing in non-English—
and as chopsticks lift the noodles
there is a momentary pause
to blow on the dangling strands,

and each pause becomes a moment
of gratitude and wonder,
like a salute to our culture,
like an offering to our history,

for although we may be strangers,
we have managed to make our way
to 82nd Avenue, in Portland,
to gather once again as a group

to enjoy life while eating noodles.

Being

by Lawson Inada

I. Asianing

While it was an honor to be asked to write a poem for Portland's pan-Asian newspaper, I didn't know what to write. What would readers think? They read the paper for coverage, issues, news ...

Then the poem appeared right under my very nose. There it was—in a bowl of relatable-reality—and the poem became a celebration of our pan-Asian, inter-related "noodle culture," and a tribute to our "noodle people," wherever we may be—for noodles are an enduring "umbilical cord" between us.

Who would we be without noodles? For instance, in my family, a slippery umbilical cord went hand-in-hand with slippery noodles, for my grandmother gave birth to my dad, in 1910, in back of a noodle shop in Watsonville, California. Which came first in that riverbank settlement—the noodle shop or the Buddhist Temple? Or, is slurping a form of worship? Is a bowl a bell?

II. Americaning

Now, as an elder myself, let me share from the "broth" of experience. And in particular, the perverse and sadistic aspect of Americana called "internment"—or, humans confined to barbed-wire "bowls"! Who were those human beings? Well, those of "Japanese ancestry," whatever that means, for among my play-mates in Jerome Camp, Arkansas, were kids of "mixed ances-try"—children of various "nationalities" and "colors," children who belonged ...

Whoever "Jerome" was, that camp made a fine fit with the Mississippi Delta region which was rich with significant history and profound presence: Slavery, the "Trail of Tears," Chinese generations, and plantation laborers from Mexico. Who was

18

"them"? Who was "us"? And though Jerome Camp was a make-shift imposition, our neighbors must have been awed by the ominous installation. Perhaps parents warned children about it, or used it as a threat; perhaps it was avoided, like a contaminated, hazardous disposal site ...

And though we may have been deprived of noodles, a commodity we had in common was music, which was in our beings, in our spirits, in the very air, to share. Thus, "internees" hummed, sang, whistled, like anyone, anywhere—pop tunes, religious songs, melodies from elsewhere ...

Also, since free-thinking musicians had seen fit to bring instruments to imprisonment, Jerome Camp was soon swinging and dancing to its own sophisticated jazz band. Why not? Bands were not banned, and jazz was truly *America's* music.

Ah, perhaps other Americans enjoyed our band. Soldiers in guard towers may have wanted to dance. Nearby residents may have appreciated our music as it wafted across fields, through trees, and in the moonlight, searchlights must have created a festive atmosphere ...

I was too young to be among swaying adults and jitterbugging teens, but a "collegiate" guy, a "hep cat" in the "bachelors' barrack," sometimes played his records for us kids. We were enthralled, by such "food for the soul"! And so it was that I became acquainted with Duke Ellington, his band playing his classic composition, *Mood Indigo*—and while it was "entertaining," it was also transfixing, music of such overwhelming beauty and power, music of a transcendent, spiritual, liberating nature ...

Where were we? And to this day, there's a mystery: How did that young man manage to have a hefty phonograph in camp? Did he carry it, along with his fragile record collection, all the way from the West Coast? If so, he must have been in "survival mode," and had his priorities.

As for me, *Mood Indigo*, to this day, is a soundtrack and *anthem*, but for contemporary tastes, I recommend a conveniently available, modern compact disc—*Duke Ellington and John Coltrane*—to enhance any bowl of nourishing noodles ...

III. Holding

Where I live—in Medford, Oregon—it's "business as usual" for me on a daily basis as I go about life as just another resident—a customer, client, whatever. And behind the steering wheel, I'm definitely a driver. And, certainly, in certain situations, I'm aware of being the "only Oriental" or perhaps the "first Asian," but: No big deal.

Or, it can be a distinction—like a former "internee" of the former "yellow peril" leaning on a redwood tree. Or, like my grandparents, making a purchase, or signing some papers, or posing proudly for a photo on a riverbank rock. Something special ...

Thus it was that, just the other ordinary day, I found a special book in the Medford Public Library. As usual, I sampled the "buffet" of the "new arrivals" section, and there it was: *Holding the Lotus to the Rock: The Autobiography of Sokei-an, America's first Zen Master*. A recent volume, 2002; I held it in my hands.

On the back cover it said: "This effort is like holding the lotus to the rock, hoping it will take root." My grandparents could relate to that, and to their contemporary who was also a common laborer, common immigrant, common "outsider"; and Sokei-an Sasaki also became a common "internee," confined to Ellis Island. Sokei-an shared common Issei values of hard work, perseverance, sacrifice, and communal spirit, but since he had also received uncommon training in the Chinese and Japanese traditions, and become fluent in English, he could have been a mainstay of our Fresno Buddhist Temple, founded in 1902.

Instead, however, on The Path, Sokei-an ventured elsewhere:

Alone in America now, I conceived the idea of going about the United States on foot. In February 1911, I crossed the Shasta Mountains through the snow into Oregon. On the hillside of the Rogue River Valley was the farm of an old friend ... . Medford was a little town, mostly living off lumber and farming ... .

Medford? It's a big town now, with a mall, but in 1911: "Everybody wore working clothes; I wore overalls all day and night.

There was nothing there—just a hick town. Medford was the only place where I found no discrimination." Thus, this questing Zen pioneer managed to find honest work in fields, orchards, and to attain janitor-rank for a tavern—as the first and only Zen spittoon-emptier in Oregon, America, and the Western Hemisphere.

He may have been an "outsider," but "inside" was the journey:

> Summer came with the month of May. I began again my practice of meditation. Every evening I used to walk along the riverbed to a rock, chiseled by the current during thousands of years. Upon its flat surface I would practice meditation through the night, my dog at my side protecting me from the snakes. The rock is still there.

Where? Behind the Taco Bell? And though Sokei-an would say, "Any rock will do!"—as a "recent arrival," I'd like to find his rock. Also, who was his "old friend"? Which makes me wonder: Who was here before me? A question well worth considering, anywhere in this Hemisphere.

As it was, Sokei-an Sasaki—American poet, sculptor, journalist, esteemed abiding presence—made his way from Medford to New York City, to found, on granite, The First Zen Institute of America. Meanwhile, I may not wear overalls, but I can walk the riverbed with my dog ...

LAWSON FUSAO INADA is an emeritus professor of English at Southern Oregon University. Since writing his debut collection of poems, *Before the War: Poems as They Happened* (1971), he has spent a career giving eloquent voice to the Japanese American internment experience. Among his many works, he has penned the poetry collections, *Legends from Camp* (1993) and *Drawing the Line* (1997), and has edited three important books of Asian American writing: *Aiiieeeee!* (1974), *The Big Aiiieeeee!* (1991), and *Only What We Could Carry* (2000). The recipient of many awards, Professor Inada earned two poetry fellowships from the National Endowment for the Arts as well as a Guggenheim Fellowship. In 2010, he concluded a four-year term as Oregon's fifth poet laureate.

Psychological Consequences of the Perpetual Foreigner Stereotype for Asian Americans

by Sapna Cheryan

"**A**re you in the Chinese Air Force?" a woman asked United States Captain Ted Lieu at an awards dinner, despite his blue U.S. Air Force uniform, captain's bars, and military insignia. This was not the first time Captain Lieu had been considered an outsider in his own country. Throughout his life, fellow Americans had expressed surprise at the fluency of his English and marveled at his fondness for professional football—hardly extraordinary qualities for a United States officer born and raised in Ohio (Lieu, 1999). Captain Lieu's identity as an Asian American, it seems, was enough to raise suspicion about whether he was American, despite a uniform that reflected an intense loyalty to America. In my research, I, along with my colleagues at the University of Washington, Stanford University, and University of California, Berkeley, investigate the psychological consequences of such stereotypes that depict Asian Americans and other non-White minorities as less than fully American.

Stereotypes of Asian Americans as "forever foreigners" (Tuan, 1998) have been pervasive throughout U.S. history and resulted in prejudice against Asian Americans (Yogeeswaran & Dasgupta, 2010). During the late 1800s and early 1900s, Chinese Americans were seen as "unassimilable" and accused of sending money that belonged in the United States back to China. During WWII, fear and intolerance reached a peak in the internment of 120,000 Japanese-Americans, 77,000 of whom were U.S.-born citizens. Historians have contrasted this treatment with German and Italian Americans, who were presumed to be far less of a threat. The stereotype can also be traced through the second half of the twentieth century. *The Daily Breeze*, a newspaper in Torrance, CA, published an article referring to Asians and Asian Americans moving into that community as an "Asian Invasion" (Shim, 1998). It is difficult to imagine a similar article on "British Invasion" that lumps together first, second, third, and fourth generation British descendents. A salient example from our recent past is the case of Wen Ho Lee, a naturalized American citizen who was imprisoned on charges of providing federal secrets to China but later freed (Lee, 2001). Besides our government, other institutions are also responsible for applying this stereotype. MSNBC's website ran a story during the 1998 Winter Olympics with the headline, "American beats out Kwan," referring to the victory of Tara Lipinksi over Michelle Kwan, an American figure skater born and raised in California (Wu, 2002).

How do these stereotypes depicting Asian Americans as less American than White Americans manifest in daily lives of Asian Americans? In our work, we have found that although Asian Americans report being and feeling American, they realize that they are not seen that way by others (Cheryan & Monin, 2005; Cheryan & Tsai, 2006). We came to term this predicament *identity denial*, defined as the tendency to have one's membership in a group doubted or unrecognized. The victims of identity denial experience a discrepancy between how they see themselves, as core group members, and how they are seen by others, as peripheral group members or as non-members. The denial of Asian Americans' American identity is instantiated through recurrent and seemingly innocent questions, such as inquiring what language they speak or where they are from. For instance, Asian Americans are more often mistaken and mislabeled as being from another country or a non-native English speaker than are White Americans (Cheryan & Monin, 2005). These questions and assumptions serve to remind Asian Americans that they differ in appearance from those who are perceived as belonging in America (Devos & Banaji, 2005) and put Asian Americans in the position of having to contend with potentially inaccurate notions about themselves.

For an Asian American who identifies as American, the exclusion that results from these stereotypes has painful and profound psychological consequences. Being rejected from a group that is an important part of one's identity interferes with a fundamental human need to belong (Baumeister & Leary, 1995). In several behavioral experiments, we demonstrated that Asian Americans who had their American identities denied—by having their English abilities questioned or their American identity directly challenged—felt more offended and angrier than Asian Americans who did not have their American identities denied (Cheryan & Monin, 2005). Like other incidents of perceived racial mistreatment, identity denial encounters are associated with greater negative emotions, higher depressive symptoms, and lower self-esteem (Chan & Mendoza-Denton, 2008; Fisher, Wallace, & Fenton, 2000; Liang, Li, & Kim, 2004).

To investigate how Asian Americans respond to identity denial, we conducted experiments in which we put Asian Americans in situations in which their American identities were doubted or unrecognized and established that Asian Americans respond to identity denial by engaging in *identity assertion*, or a tendency to boost their American identity to prove they belong as Americans (Cheryan & Monin, 2005). Asian Americans who were confronted with a question indicating that their American identity might be in doubt (i.e., "Do you speak English?") spent more time recalling American cultural knowledge as a means to verify their identity as Americans (Cheryan & Monin, 2005). In contrast, White Americans, who are perceived as fitting the image of a prototypical American (Devos & Banaji, 2005), did not change their behaviors. In another experiment, Asian Americans who encountered an assumption that they were not American reported leading a more American lifestyle (e.g., having American friends, playing American sports) than Asian Americans who did not have their American identities denied. Interestingly, Asian Americans did not invoke greater feelings of pride in the U.S. as a way to assert their American identity, perhaps because it may be difficult to feel pride in a country that is excluding them from that identity.

More recently, we have extended our work on identity denial to examine potential health consequences of being the victim of these stereotypes and found that identity denial has negative implications for the health of Asian Americans (Guendelman, Cheryan, & Monin, 2011; Wang, Siy, & Cheryan, 2011). Asian Americans who had their American identities denied chose unhealthier American foods (e.g., hamburger) over more nutritious Asian foods (e.g., sushi) in an attempt to prove their American identities (Guendelman et al., 2011). Trading a traditional diet and lifestyle for a standard American diet and lifestyle may be a strategy, albeit a potentially harmful one, that Asian Americans use to prove to others that they belong in America.

Look around the U.S., and it becomes clear that Americans cut across the color spectrum. Yet when asked to picture an American, many people immediately conjure up the image of someone White. As a consequence, Asian Americans are seen as less American and have their identities as Americans questioned on a regular basis. We find in our work, using a social-psychological perspective and corresponding behavioral experiments, that Asian Americans are not passive in the face of such threats to their American identities but react by altering their behavior in the face of these threats, sometimes to their own detriment. Doing away with stereotypes that racialize certain Americans as less American than others will be important to ensuring the health and well-being of Asian Americans.

For more information about this work, see the following research articles:

Cheryan, S., & Monin, B. (2005). "Where are you really from?": Asian Americans and identity denial. *Journal of Personality and Social Psychology, 89*, 717-730.

Cheryan, S., & Tsai, J. L. (2006). Ethnic Identity. In F. T. Leong, A. G. Inman, A. Ebreo, L. Yang, L. Kinoshita & M. Fu (Eds.), *Handbook of Asian American Psychology*. Thousand Oaks, CA: Sage.

Guendelman, M., Cheryan, S., & Monin, B. (2011). Fitting in but getting fat: Identity threat as an explanation for dietary decline among U.S. immigrant groups. *Psychological Science, 22*, 959-967.

REFERENCES

Chan, W., & Mendoza-Denton, R. (2008). Status-based rejection sensitivity among Asian Americans: Implications for psychological distress. *Journal of Personality, 76*, 1317-1346.

Cheryan, S., & Monin, B. (2005). "Where are you really from?": Asian Americans and identity denial. *Journal of Personality and Social Psychology, 89*, 717-730.

Cheryan, S., & Tsai, J. L. (2006). Ethnic Identity. In F. T. Leong, A. G. Inman, A. Ebreo, L. Yang, L. Kinoshita & M. Fu (Eds.), *Handbook of Asian Psychology*. Thousand Oaks, CA: Sage.

Devos, T., & Banaji, M. R. (2005). American = White? *Journal of Personality and Social Psychology, 88*, 447-466.

Fisher, C. B., Wallace, S. A., & Fenton, R. E. (2000). Discrimination distress during adolescence. *Journal of Youth and Adolescence, 29*, 679-695.

Guendelman, M., Cheryan, S., & Monin, B. (2011). Fitting in but getting fat: Identity threat as an explanation for dietary decline among U.S. immigrant groups. *Psychological Science, 22, 959-967*.

Lee, W. H. (2001). *My country versus me: The first-hand account by the Los Alamos scientist who was falsely accused of being a spy*. New York: Hyperion.

Liang, C. T. H., Li, L. C., & Kim, B. S. K. (2004). The Asian American Racism-Related Stress Inventory: Development, factor analysis, reliability, and validity. *Journal of Counseling Psychology, 51*, 103-114.

Lieu, T. W. (1999, June 19). Are you in the Chinese Air Force? *Washington Post*, p. A19.

Shim, D. (1998). From Yellow Peril through Model Minority to Renewed Yellow Peril. *Journal of Communication Inquiry, 22*, 385.

Tuan, M. (1998). *Forever Foreigners or Honorary Whites?: The Asian Ethnic Experience Today*: Rutgers University Press.

Wang, J., Siy, J. O., & Cheryan, S. (2011). Racial discrimination and mental health among Asian American youth. In F. T. L. Leong, L. Juang, D. B. Qin & H. E. Fitzgerald (Eds.), *Asian American and Pacific Islander Children and Mental Health Volume 1: Development and Context* (pp. pp. 219-242). Santa Barbara, CA: Greenwood.

Wu, F. (2002). *Yellow: Race in America Beyond Black and White*. New York: Basic Books.

Yogeeswaran, K., & Dasgupta, N. (2010). Will the "real" American please stand up? The effect of implicit national prototypes on discriminatory behavior and judgments. *Personality and Social Psychology Bulletin, 36*, 1332.

SAPNA CHERYAN is an assistant professor of psychology at the University of Washington. Her research interests include identity, stereotypes, and prejudice, and she has published articles on stereotype threat and strategies of belonging to social groups in journals such as the *Journal of Personality & Social Psychology* and *Psychological Science*. Her awards include the National Science Foundation CAREER Award and  the American Psychological Association Dissertation Research Award. She received her Ph.D. in social psychology from Stanford University in 2007.

All Orientals Look Alike

An Installation by Roberta May Wong
Black and white portraits, woven composite image,
funerary setting,
6' x 2' x 4'
1984

ARTIST STATEMENT:

All Orientals Look Alike, set in a funerary setting, mourns the loss of identity imposed by stereotypes while, at the same time, shows the collective power of individuals to shatter those stereotypes by using the symbol of the central interwoven image, a composite of the four individual portraits.

Available for exhibition: Contact rwong129@gmail.com

All-American

An Installation by Roberta Wong
Braided hair, Chinese cleaver, round chopping block,
stainless steel table and rubber floor mat
36" x 36" x 42.25", 2003

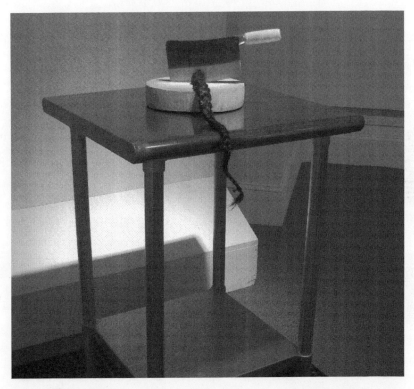

ARTIST STATEMENT:

All-American pays homage to all hyphenated Americans, immigrants who have sacrificed a part of their personal identity to become American. Their loss, sometimes visible, often not, is symbolic of the human need to survive, adapting to new environments via change in appearance, social practice, and/or hidden cultural traits. All-American utilizes visual elements of the artist's Chinese heritage but mourns our collective loss of cultural identities.

Chinks, III

An Installation by Roberta Wong
Student desk, world map, books
8' x 8' x 5', 2004

ARTIST STATEMENT:

Chinks, III is a statement about the political bias that existed during the Cold War period affecting the educational environment I experienced as a student of the 60s and 70s. As a young student, I sat at my desk and looked up at the big yellow spot on the map—China, a void in the topic of social studies beyond the singular reference to Marco Polo. As a Chinese American, my cultural identity was at risk, my self-esteem overshadowed by potential shame, as China was a Communist country—the enemy. Sympathies could be interpreted as treasonous, unprotected by fame or fortune, as Hollywood personalities—blacklisted—would discover.

Chinks, III is a wall of books whose foundation is built upon the very set of encyclopedias purchased by my father, an immigrant who came to America with his father in the late 20s. He built his life with hard labor in Chinese kitchens and grocery stores, having only a fifth grade education. Many immigrants came to get an American education. Multiple sets of encyclopedias reference many lives and many families seeking world-class knowledge. But in the classroom during the 50s and 60s, old school textbooks with a nationalistic perspective were full of chink—void of the histories of Native American, African American, Hispanic American, Asian American and women's history. Contemporary book titles represent various efforts of modern historians to fill the holes, to broaden the knowledge and perspective of man, and to bring cultural understanding to enhance our place in this global environment.

Chinks, III is the third in a series of wall installations entitled Chinks. The series deals with the issue of race and racism from the perspective of an Asian American.

As an Asian American, I hear the word "Chink" and can't help but think of the offensiveness of that word and the derogatory meaning it implies.

As an Artist, I reply, "the truth can be offensive! And, if we choose to ignore the reality of human bias, arrogance and cruelty, can we hope to find our humanity?"

Chinks, III comes from the core of my being, not as a person of Chinese descent, not as an American, but as a human being, indebted to those who came before me, those who stand at the front lines, and those on the mountain top, holding the light of dawn, leading us into a new day.

Red, White & Blue

An Installation by Roberta May Wong
Galvanized aluminum shelf, hooks, 3 soiled aprons, 64 laundry
packets, 5' x 6' x 1', 2004

ARTIST STATEMENT:

Red, White & Blue is a tribute to the honest profession and hard
labor of new immigrants. Working for the American dream, their
passion, idealism, or sacrifice can be worn thin by questions
of allegiance by "true" Americans who measure the degree of
patriotism by the color of one's skin. The scrutiny faced by
immigrants, even after a lifetime, and generations, of living in
America raises the question—How Red? How White? How Blue?
 The occupations of Chinese immigrants as cooks or laundry

workers typified the early Asian American stereotype. Freshly laundered aprons stack neatly above the soiled aprons—faintly stained to symbolize the sacrifice of those who toiled long hours to provide for their families, many separated by immigration laws that kept them oceans apart.

Red, White & Blue also juxtaposes the numerical reference of the number 64 (hexagrams of the I-Ching) and the trilogy to underscore the cultural and philosophical relationships between a life defined by fate and faith.

Available for exhibition: Contact rwong129@gmail.com

ROBERTA MAY WONG is a native of Portland, Oregon. She received a bachelor of arts degree in sculpture from Portland State University (1983). She has exhibited in Oregon and Washington. Recent exhibitions include Interstate Firehouse Cultural Center, Portland, OR; Evergreen State College, WA; Portland Community College, Sylvania Campus, Portland, OR; and The Wing Luke Asian Museum's touring exhibition, Beyond Talk: Redrawing Race, to South Seattle Community College of Art and Phinney Center Art Gallery in Seattle, WA. Her work is published in Surviving Myths (Deakin University, Australia, 1990 & 2000) and The Forbidden Stitch: An Anthology of Asian American Women Artists (Calyx, Corvallis, Oregon) which won the American Book Award, 1990.

From 1985-1988 and 1995-2004, Wong was gallery director at the Interstate Firehouse Cultural Center. She also produced and curated independent community exhibitions and served on the board of NW Artists Workshop (1984-1987) and the McKenzie River Gathering Foundation (1985-1989). Wong also served on panels for the Metropolitan Art Commission/ Regional Arts & Culture Council, Oregon Arts Commission, TriMet's Public Art Committee, and Portland State University's Walk of the Heroine project.

We Will Take What We Can Get

by Matthew Salesses

1.

I've just pitched the idea to Cathreen and she does not look happy about it.

"You think I'm funny character?" she says.

"I think we both are. Look at all the ridiculous things that have been happening to us," I say. I tell her I'll write the essay in real-time.

"Give me money," she says. She calls her sister to complain.

2.

This started when I slammed her hand in the door—two days ago. Today her hair caught fire in the bathtub. I had filled the tub for her and lit candles to relax her from the bad mood she had woken up in. The pain from the injury, she says, is shocking, though she doesn't mean this like surprising, she means it like electricity. The doctor says she has to wear a soft cast and keep her arm in a sling for two weeks; her hand has swollen up and, last we saw it, was badly bruised. When I tell people what I have done, I know they are thinking I beat her. Other people's ideas frighten me.

3.

Now she comes into the room and asks, "Are you going to use my name? You going to write down everything I say? You didn't get a permission from me." She says her family will read it, though they will have to struggle through translating it into Korean.

I tell her art has to be honest.

"Let me read first before you put it," she says. I read it to her.

"Not funny," she says, "your story."

4.

During the day, I take her to the hospital to get a second opinion on her injury. The first doctor asked her to stay in the infirmary for a week. While we're waiting, a nurse pushes a cart into my toe and doesn't apologize.

"Ouch," I say.

"That's ouch?" Cathreen asks.

"I don't mean it's as bad as yours."

She squeezes my hand between the embedded bones of my thumb and forefinger. "Even that's ouch?" she says.

5.

We met more than three years ago, when I first came to Korea to teach English. I was born in this country but adopted. So I'm Korean only not. Now we're engaged and living in her mother's house while her mother is in America.

The day of the door-slamming, we were fighting about the future. Cathreen has always told me to be more careful with doors—which, a fact I like, are called "moon" in Korean.

6.

After I finish work, I meet my beleaguered love at a Korean department store. She's had a haircut and keeps asking if I like it. Her hair has always been long and beautiful; now it's short and makes her look a bit like a doll and a bit like a 13-year-old. It surrounds her face in a bell-shape and new bangs even out above her eyes.

"Do I look cute?" she asks.

"Okay," I say. "I like it."

We watch a Chinese movie about two music students who fall in love, the girl about to die, called *Secret*. We aren't able to finish it because she feels sick to her stomach—the new medicine is too strong, and she says she is depressed about her hair.

7.

If I rethink publishing this essay, I suppose I am a little worried. This whole project will test me on the asshole-o-meter, as I've already done so much to hurt her I can't say anything now that could be taken the wrong way.

8.

Cathreen makes me catch the cat and hold him while she brushes him. "Maybe it's time Boise gets a haircut, too," I say.

She doesn't answer.

9.

I dream of doing something I've always wanted to do. In the morning I can't remember what it was. I wake to find Cathreen's face beside me. Usually she tutors at this time. She says I need to do her lesson for her—she's too dizzy.

I nod that I will and then roll over in bed.

"You need to go now," she says. "It's time issue."

I've obligated myself to do this for her, by causing her pain. "Okay," I say, "I'll go. Just don't bother me. I can wake up on my own."

I'm only a few minutes late.

10.

I teach her student about the growth of San Francisco, a subject I don't expect him to be interested in. He says he wants to go there and find gold. "There's no more left," I tell him. "They've found it all."

11.

Later, at her sister's house, Cathreen asks what I wrote yesterday. When I read it to her, she says I'm making her look bad. "I'm not," I say. "I'm making myself look bad."

She voices a few complaints. "Where's the part about how I'm hero?" she asks. What she means is we've been watching this television series about people who develop superpowers—she says hers is knowing the future, how she's been buying wide-sleeved, loose-fitting clothes for years and now they're easy to fit on and off around her cast.

I write what she asks.

12.

Someone from home asks how much of Cathreen's hair burned. A lot or just a little singing, he asks, as in from the verb "to singe," not "to sing."

13.

I sit by my nephew and write. Cathreen's sister had a baby five months ago, an active thing with a big voice who thinks he has two mothers.

"Hello," I say. He starts to cry. He doesn't remember me.

When Cathreen tells her sister what I'm writing, they say it's "evidence."

14.

After work I come home to more bad news: Cathreen has chipped her tooth. I tell her this has to go in the essay. "Some people I guess won't believe all what happened to me," she says. I don't believe it myself. This is the kind of thing that wouldn't seem honest in fiction.

15.

We go back to see the rest of the Chinese movie, *Secret*, and it turns out the girl wasn't dying. The secret she was keeping was that she was a time traveler from twenty years in the past. The movie goes on from here for another forty minutes.

I saw a Korean film once about two jesters who perform for the king. The first half of the movie is comedy. Everyone dies in the end.

I think about Cathreen's hand, her hair, her tooth, the movie. Something here seems significant.

16.

Here are some notes about this project, good and bad:

First, how the format allows a simulation of real life—good and bad.

Second, how I've censored myself—bad.

Third, how what I write affects what I write—good and bad. (This last one, for example: if Cathreen reads what I write that changes what happens, and what I write, next, not like working with a set past.)

17.

In the morning, I fry eggs and bring Cathreen her medicine; I tutor her student again; I come home and wash her hair. I cook the rice with too much water and it sticks together in one big lump, refusing to come apart. When the grains are too loose, Cathreen calls it "flying rice," an expression in Korean.

18.

As I write the dogs are scratching at the floor in the living room. Some leftover of their primal urge to dig holes.

19.

I don't know how much longer I can write this. It seems like I'm only looking out for the next bad thing that will happen.

I get a package from home and it's full of wet books and paperwork. Something inside is leaking.

20.

One of the teachers where I work is leaving and they have a cake for him. He says he is going to travel around Eastern Europe for a while. I tell him when he's in Prague to go to the top of Petr'i'n Hill, where lovers meet, and drink at the monastery there. "Best beer in the world," I say. I know he will not remember this. I don't say, "Have a good life."

21.

I pick up Cathreen. On the way back we make a U-turn I think is unnecessary. I am unreasonably angry about this.

We both know who will win the next thousand fights.

22.

I wake up at 3 in the afternoon. There is feces on the floor—the dogs have no respect. Sometimes after Cathreen and I make up I think about the woman in Grace Paley's "Wants." (Hello, my life.) How sad.

23.

I will stop writing now. It is time for Cathreen's medicine. Later her stomach will hurt as much, it seems, as her hand, though I know this can't be true.

24.

For dinner we go to a beef restaurant we tried once and liked, and on the way Cathreen says we can stop by her sister's house afterward. The restaurant is closed, but as we settle into the car again, her sister calls to say she had a feeling she should ask where we were.

Cathreen has told me before how they have a psychic connection, like twins. I remember the night she had stomach cramps and woke me up screaming, and in the morning, she called her sister and it turned out the baby had been born.

We eat at their house and watch a movie afterward. I walk with her brother-in-law to pick out the DVD. He says something in Korean, and something else, and then tugs on my earmuffs, and we walk out in the rain not understanding each other.

25.

Christmas shopping. Why is it so hard to pick out something other people will like? I don't know whether I ask this as a personal question or a human one.

26.

The dogs and cat fight like dogs and cats. Cathreen looks at dog-training devices online. The machines look complicated. Here's one for multiple-dog houses: a bark is amplified at dog pitch, and the other canines, annoyed, beat up on the first one to teach him a lesson.

I think.

The reviews do not sound promising.

27.

Cathreen seems to have lost interest in the essay. Her hand is healing. She didn't take medicine all day yesterday. Instead she stayed in bed and surfed the Internet.

She came out once to watch TV and dug her nails into my skin without noticing. I yelled, frightening her out of her reverie. She went back into the bedroom. Later we both apologized and went to sleep. That was the weekend.

28.

When I slammed the door on her I was trying to storm out of the room and make a scene. I didn't know her hand was there. This doesn't make it any better.

I am shipwrecked on an island of guilt.

29.

A few days ago, her mother asked her to go to the family fortune teller and retrieve their fortunes for 2009. My luck was supposed to get better in December.

This is the same fortune teller who thought I had died when I was two, when Cathreen went to see him about us getting married. He said my life in Korea had ended then. I was adopted when I was two. He said we're a good match if I'm still alive.

Or maybe this was another fortune teller—I can't remember.

30.

I think "Shipwrecked" would be a good title. We're wandering around picking up the fragments of what was broken when her hand almost was. We'll build a shelter here against cannibals and bad luck.

31.

During the day Cathreen complains that, since she started healing, I haven't treated her as nicely as before. I help her put on make-up before she goes to my workplace to convince my boss to let me have Christmas off.

There are so many things girls can do to their faces. Things that look dangerous. She runs a pencil across her eye and I try not to make any sudden movements.

32.

At night, I come home and she's despondent on the bed, her cast off. The sides of her fingers are white and pruned. "Skin's off," she says. They look skinny from the top and fat from the side—the swelling is mostly on her palm, as if she has another hand inside the first. We talk about how we've never seen a bruised palm before.

It's hard to create an arc when life keeps starting us back at the beginning.

33.

We buy hats for Christmas while we purchase another bandage to wrap her hand. Hers is a polar bear. Mine a raccoon. I am inappropriately excited. Maybe it's compensation.

I know in some ways this whole experience will help us. I will always be more careful with her.

Or maybe it will only help me. But maybe that's enough.

34.

She goes to sleep before me. I have a beer and stare at the computer. I stare at this essay but don't write anything. When I enter the bedroom she is sprawled across the mattress. I kiss her on the temple. I worry.

35.

In the morning we wear our hats to her student's apartment, and the two boys there both have animal hats as well.

36.

We go to the hospital afterward.

The doctor says it will take her another month to regain movement in her hand. He shines some sort of laser on her. My eyes hurt to watch.

"Don't look," I tell her.

"I'm not," she says. She calls her sister and I lie down on the bed across from her.

37.

I want to write here that this will be a good day, because I will make it one. I decide to write this. I write, "I want to write here that this will be a good day, because I will make it one. I decide to write this. I write . . . " But I stop before it gets stupid.

I'm thinking about self-fulfilling prophecies.

38.

At work I pull a girl out of class and tell her to talk to a Korean teacher about her behavior. She comes back embittered and straightened out. I'm surprised how well this has worked.
She'll forget it by the next class. Both of us hate the material.

39.

I rush home to pick Cathreen up for dinner. I've planned an expensive place on a hill that overlooks the ocean.

"Someone's blocking us," she says as I help her with her clothes, fitting them carefully around the cast. I ask her to wear the boots I bought for her. "More bad luck."

We take the elevator down and a produce truck is blocking three cars, one of which is ours. This is at 10:40 and the restaurant closes at 11.

The security guard calls the guy, goes up to his apartment, talks to the wife, the wife promises to call the guy. We see the guy walk toward us, but he doesn't stop. He hurries for the elevator as we call to him.

We go back to the security guard. I am ready to key this guy's truck.

The security guard calls the guy, the guy comes down, tells some ridiculous lies, finally moves his truck for us, then drives it back in to block the other cars.

This almost ruins our night.

40.

Since we get to the restaurant a little past 11, they let us eat in the café. Cathreen is furious at the guy and I'm tired from work and drove like an idiot to get here, stopping in the middle of the street at a red light. But the food is delicious.

41.

I think I can keep her happy.

42.

Cathreen wasn't able to convince my boss to let me have Christmas off. We talk about whether I'd be willing to threaten to walk away.

I might, but I'm scared for the future.

We need the money for when we go to America, which we will in March, if we get the visa, to get married. Then we will live in Boston. I will finish my novel. Everything will work out.

You see, we have plans.

43.

After the restaurant, my responsibilities as heavy as a drowning body I can either leave or rescue, I say, "Life is a bitch."

"No, it's not," says my love.

"It's an expression," I tell her.

44.

My Christmas Eve lesson is about hibernating animals. Woodland frogs, I find out, hibernate under leaves, their bodies freezing and then thawing out in spring.

The kids are not as amazed by this as I am.

We talk about monsters. We talk about things that scare them. I tell them again about dolls that look too much like people. But I keep thinking of frogs coming back to life.

45.

When I get home Cathreen has a new cast. It's small and blue and looks like one of those knee braces except for it's on her hand. Compared to the last piece it's adorable. It allows her fingers to breathe.

She says in the morning she washed her hand and dead skin flaked off like rain.

46.

These events have me thinking about the New Year, starting fresh. Cathreen comes in and says not to write about our Christmas.

47.

Before midnight we deliver presents for her tutoring kids, calling ourselves Santa's helpers. The two boys have plastic bows that shoot arrows with suction cups on the end. I shoot one boy in the stomach. I tell them not to shoot their teachers, and they listen.

48.

We tell my boss I'm not coming on Christmas and it's up to him whether he wants to fire me. "It's God's day," Cathreen says. That's right. We'll leave it up to God.

49.

I get fired.

50.

When I wake up, Cathreen comes and lies down next to me. I slept in the other room again. She says she's sorry she was cranky.

Her palm hurts. But she can move her fingers, if only a few centimeters.

51.

Now she calls me into the other room. The cat is eating the dog food. This, we figure, must be why they hate him.

He is supposed to be dieting to fit on the plane to America.

52.

In the afternoon, Cathreen sits down and reads what I have written since last she checked. She asks, "Why didn't you writing about our Christmas?"

"Okay," I say, "I will. You told me not to." I should have stopped with "I will."

Here's what happened on Christmas:

We had a spat on the way to her sister's house, but I figured the baby would cheer her up. "Uri Ji-hwan," she calls him, "our Ji-hwan," though he is only our nephew.

She decorated a cake and made cookies and I tried to make eggnog but failed.

After eating sweets we went to a Christian university high on an island mountain. Lights were strung up everywhere and people filled the streets and you could see the city below.

"Do you feel like it's Christmas now?" Cathreen asked as we walked through a candy-cane forest. "Was it worth it?" I said it was.

We walked to the car, and I felt my tenderness for her and hers for me like a thinning of air, making it hard to breathe.

For dinner we ate raw fish and fried chicken and drank failed eggnog and soju and beer.

53.

Cathreen says, "Describe me as wise and sweet and kind." I promise I will. This is the truth: Cathreen is wise and sweet and kind.

54.

I clean up after the dogs again. Before Cathreen was hurt she used to do this. Now I can appreciate how much she loves those dogs. They aren't my dogs, though. We've only just met.

55.

I teach her students how to cut paper snowflakes. At first the littler one doesn't get it: how if you snip the edges everything falls apart. I tell him he has to cut out the parts where the paper can support the loss.

56.

Last night her hand buzzed with pain but I had a headache and couldn't be sympathetic.

This morning I woke up with the headache still. Usually the pain goes away after sleep.

57.

I keep thinking back to that movie, *Secret*. There are things that didn't make sense, things that do not add up. The shock of reconfiguring what kind of movie I was watching made these things seem as if they didn't matter, but they do.

58.

Meanwhile I try not to think about what the doctor will say today, how long he will say she has to stay in her cast, how long he will say before our life can go back to the way it was.

Cathreen is wise and sweet and kind.

59.

In the morning, or really, afternoon, we go to the bank to transfer some money home. The exchange rate flickers every few minutes, my savings becoming more and less before my eyes.

"1287," I say. "1278." I don't say anything when it goes up over 1300 again.

The economy is so uncaring.

60.

Cathreen says that in section 43, I didn't say, "It's an expression," but I wrote that I did. Maybe I was just thinking this. Maybe I wanted to think she didn't understand when she did. I think, even, that I didn't say, "Life is a bitch," but, "Life sucks." Simply, unambiguously, enough.

61.

This morning, Cathreen's elder student was supposed to read but only spoke the words as he had memorized them. I tried to make him look at the letters, but he kept repeating mistakes that only existed in his head. How can you fight what isn't really there?

62.

We see another movie. The movie is called *Innocent Voices*, in

Spanish, and is set in El Salvador during the civil war. For the first half, everything seems so true I almost forget it's based on a real story, but then the boy becomes a man.

When the credits roll, Cathreen says, "We have a happy life, right?" The family in the movie lost their house, watched their friends die, were almost killed by children bearing arms. I should have been thinking about this in the same way.

63.

At home, Cathreen lies in bed and reads the news. The world is stressing her out. I wish the world would quit it.

So much has happened in the last two weeks. Her hand, her hair, our good days and bad, Christmas. Israel is bombing Palestine.

I wish we would learn.

64.

In the morning, we wake up early to take out the recycling from the past two weeks and in the parking lot, boxes are piled high like the ruins of cardboard castles. Cathreen says everyone is cleaning for the New Year. I think about Italians throwing plates out of windows to keep away the spirits of their pasts—something like that. Tomorrow is the arbitrary day we say the earth begins another orbit around the sun.

With 2009 comes the clean slate we set for ourselves.

We will take what we can get.

65.

If this seems a natural ending, the last day of the year, I didn't plan it. All experiments, great or small, must end.

As I drive Cathreen to work, something I say causes a storm to pass across her face, and I know I haven't been fair to her. I've been too harsh on her character, and perhaps on my own, as I am prone to do. Except this is real life, not fiction.

"Don't writing about me anymore," she says. "I'm getting frustrated." I stare blankly ahead. "Now you're going to writing: *Cathreen says, 'Don't writing about me anymore. I'm getting frustrated,'* right?" I can't help but think this is the perfect ending. I don't want to make her angry, but our honest reactions, in injury and in recuperation, are what I've been trying to capture—before the heightened tragic state eventually peters out.

 MATTHEW SALESSES was born in Korea and adopted at age two. He lives in Boston with his wife, new baby, and cats. He is the author of *The Last Repatriate* (Nouvella Books) and *Our Island of Epidemics* (PANK). His fiction and nonfiction have been published in *Glimmer Train, Koream, American Short Fiction, Witness, The Literary Review,* and many other publications. He writes a column, "Love, Recorded," about his marriage for the Good Men Project, where he is also fiction editor. Find him online here: matthewsalesses.com.

"sex myths"
by Min K. Kang

I want to know what you think
when you hear this—

my boyfriend's cousins asked
if my vagina ran horizontally
because Orientals are
queens of backwardness.
they also asked if I was
good in bed but
        good in bed I was not.

he didn't know how to answer
so here I am, asking you.

* * *

is there a more
learned way to
suck someone so
I won't look like
I'm bowing
because I'm so
grateful for
white cock?

* * *

if European women are women
and American women, childlike,
then are Korean women
forever infantile? the country values
virginal wives, blushing or putting

out

on command.

they have a name for women
who straddle this
dichotomy—*nae soong*.
the act of acting.

Wang nae soong or
big *nae soong*,
a faker.

rejecting
the childbride act
gets you other names. *Kka*—
or the sound
of a chestnut being
cracked open. a flower,
bloomed. legs,
spread.

MIN K. KANG was born in Busan, South Korea and was raised in Texas. For the past two years, she has worked with America Reads, a federally funded program to increase literacy and to help foster a love for reading at West Portal Elementary School in San Francisco.

Her work is featured in *Asia Literary Review, Santa Clara Review, Transfer Magazine,* and the forthcoming anthology called *Pho for Life: A Melting Pot of Thoughts.*

She has attended Texas A&M University and San Francisco State University and will start her MFA in poetry at Louisiana State University this fall.

Dog Muncher

by Beth Kaufka

We call this Girls Night Out, a name we should change because the point of the whole once-a-month ordeal is to find guys, and one of us, if it's a successful night, ends up ditching the girls completely. We dress up in clothes we'd be ashamed to wear around our parents, low on top, short on the bottom. Tiff always dresses for the most success, which means, the sluttiest. Tonight, she wears a strapless dress that dips in a deep V in front. It's held up with a little luck, perhaps some prayer, and double-sided tape. It's black, the dress I had wanted, tried on, and left crumpled on the floor of the dressing room because it made me look like a fresh-off-the-boat Asian prostitute. Too long for my body, the dress's curves hung in all the wrong places, the bottom hem coming mid-knee, the perfect length for schoolmarms in thick, nude pantyhose. Tiff's stacked in the back, as you wouldn't expect from such a white, white girl. My short Asian butt sits flat and low on my back like a half-empty, loose fitting fanny pack.

Tiff's just arrived at my apartment to pick me up for the evening. She always picks me up first; it takes Vickie longer to get ready—after all, Vickie is the weather girl. The three of us, infamous news station gals. I watch Tiff's exposed long legs as she stomps snow onto the doormat. "So, what's up, my little yellow monkey?" she greets me. I make monkey calls as I always do. Our terms of endearment tend to be racial epithets, our way of deflating them. Inside jokes only we're allowed to make.

I hand her a rum and coke. She clicks across my hardwoods in red cowboy boots. Mr. It's A Baby!, my Jack Russell terrier, yaps and bites at her heels until she bends down to pet him. Then, he piddles on the floor.

"Damn it, Mr. It's A Baby!" Tiff says, pushing him away with her foot.

"Your dog," I remind her. Tiff bought Mr. It's A Baby! a few years ago, after we graduated and each moved into our own apartments. She saw him in the window of the Pet Pen, took him home and threw him a baby shower—with invitations and gift registry—really just an excuse to have a party. During the event, she held a contest to name the dog. The wining name came from the invitation. But, just one week after the big party, she showed up at my door.

"If you take him," she said, dog carrier in her one hand, and duffle bag of dog food and rubber balls in the other, "you can have him for free. But you have to promise not to turn him into chop suey."

Ha. Either way, I always wanted my own dog.

I met Tiff in the dorms seven years ago when she was dating Izuru, a Japanese exchange student, who I actually sort of met before I met Tiff when he tried to speak to me in Japanese in the dorm lobby. I ignored him on the way up the elevator and down the hall. I'd have probably been nicer to him if I knew he was headed to the room across from mine. When Tiff, wrapped in nothing but a towel, opened the door for him, her long blond hair wet and bound up in a single chopstick, we smiled at each other. Though she lived across the hall, I'd actually never seen her before. She kissed Izuru, which impressed me. I'd never known a white girl who dated Asian guys. But, then again, I guess I haven't known many Asian guys in the first place—and I'm Asian, sort of.

Tiff teases me when I tell people I'm Korean-American. "No, she's not," she corrects me. "She's Adopted-American." It's one of her favorite jokes, though I've never really thought it funny. But, it's true. I don't have much claim to any Koreanness. I once registered for a Tae Kwon Do class in college, but after a week, dropped it for Hip Hop Aerobics.

I wipe up Mr. It's A Baby!'s pee and we're out the door to SEEN, a new club that's just opened on the Eastside of Detroit. On our way, we stop to pick up Vickie in Tiff's Jetta. Vickie also works at the news station with us. We're quite the threesome. I'm a reporter, Tiff's an editor, and Vickie's the weather girl.

Just outside SEEN, the Jetta's heater blasts while we fix our lip-gloss in the rear view mirror, fluff our hair, compliment each other. You look great! No, you look great! No, you look great! We take off our coats. I exchange my snow boots for a shiny pair of high heels. Tiff passes a flask of Southern Comfort to warm us before we step outside. In unison, we snap our handbags shut, open the doors, and step out of the car into dirty snow. We walk toward the line of people waiting to get into SEEN. Wind blows our skirts tight against our legs. We try to position our faces in the wind so it doesn't ruin our hair. We're like a team, advancing side by side, working our way across the field. We wonder if anyone is watching. We wonder if we'll win.

At the door, Vickie flirts with the bouncer who recognizes her as the weather girl. She shows off her telestrating skills on a pretend map, ushering in a storm with the wave of her hand. "Look out," she says. "There's a wave of high pressure blowing in from the south that'll keep temperatures hot and conditions wet."

"Vickie," Tiff says, "you're such a slut!" She slaps Vickie on the ass and the sound snaps off her tight skirt. They toss their arms around each other's waists and start to bump their hips together. Then their butts. They hop and turn and bump. I walk past, trying to ignore the show, and they simultaneously slap me where I wish a real butt was.

In the club, we get drinks and dance until Vickie points across the room to two white guys and one Asian guy sipping their beers at a tall round table. "Hey, check them out," she says, "Van Damme, Kevin Bacon, and Jackie Chan. Perfect. One for each of us."

"Shut up," I say. I try to grab her arm, but she takes off toward them.

The first guy, the big one, doesn't fit into his t-shirt, like he thinks his little brother's t-shirt shows off his muscles better than one of his own. He's also wearing factory-ripped jeans that flare out ever so slightly at the ankle. His goatee is crooked, leaning off to the right of his cleft chin. In the streaming lights, the gel in his hair shines like wet plastic. The second one does sort of look like Kevin Bacon, *A Few Good Men*-era. His blond hair scoops up and out from his long forehead for a clear view of his pinchy face. He's got on a silver and gold polka-dotted shirt, unbuttoned to his sternum. When he runs his hand through his hair, his Kanji tattoo peeks out from beneath his sleeve, including its English translation: Wisdom. Soon Vickie is grabbing Kevin Bacon's arm and tugging him toward the dance floor. She gives Jackie Chan a few quick pokes in the shoulder and points at me. He looks. I walk away—quickly—in the other direction. I need a drink.

I squeeze in between a couple of people and try to make eye contact with the bartender and I do, but it doesn't matter. There's a rowdy bunch of frat boys banging on the bar, ordering each other shots. I wait, my view oscillating between frat boys, the bartender, and Vickie talking with our male counterparts.

"Foxy lady!" One of the frat boys shouts at me over the music. He high-fives one of the passing guys.

"Gross." I begin to walk away. My drink can wait.

"What?" he says, "Hey, are you Japanese?"

"No. Why? Are you?"

"What are you then?" He rubs one finger up and down my forearm. I look down at my arm and back up at him.

"I'm done with you," I say and flick his hand away as hard as I can.

"Sorry for living."

"I, too, am sorry you're living."

He looks at me like I'm suddenly the ugliest person he's ever seen. "Dog-Muncher-Bitch," he says and takes off before I can shoot back a rebuttal. I'm rendered speechless. I can't even get out an easy "asshole" because I'm so impressed with the slur. Dog Muncher? Honestly, I think it's a good one. I have to admit that. It's got all the elements of a good slur: an ignorant stereotype, humor, and creative wording. My senior year in college, I dated this black guy for a while. I met him in an Afro-Caribbean Literature course; a militant Black Nationalist dating an Asian chick. We got a charge out of it. I never told him my folks are white, that I'm adopted, grew up in a mostly white neighborhood. Anyway, we used to lie in bed at night, saying every single racist epithet that came to mind, laughing hysterically. Our favorites: Africoon, Rice-Rice-Baby, Porch Monkey, Ching-Chong-Chopstick, Negroid, Egg Roll Hole.

We'd laugh and laugh.

Sometimes, there's not much more you can do.

I get my drink and work my way through the crowd back to my friends, where it's safe. Tiff and Vickie are standing in a puff of smoke; they're sharing a Newport Light cigarette and talking with T-Shirt Man, Kevin Bacon, and Jackie Chan, the five of them laughing like old friends. When I arrive, they go quiet. Tiff nods to Vickie who nods to T-shirt Man who nods to Kevin Bacon, and then they leave me with Jackie Chan, alone and awkward. They walk off in the direction of more drinks.

Jackie Chan and I stand there a few seconds, just looking at each other, like we're in shock that our friends would do such a thing. He's got on plain dark Levis and a black, cotton button-up shirt, top button undone, revealing a white t-shirt underneath. His hair is short and neat, shaved down to a quarter inch of jet-black fuzz. More of a Chow Yun Fat than a Jackie Chan, if I have to pin him down to Hollywood. He's quite handsome. He smells like sandalwood soap.

"I'm Eddie Chin."

I shake his hand. "Abby Miller."

And then I imagine the interaction goes like this: He says, "It's very nice to meet you," to which I would say something like: "They're trying to set us up because we're both Asian, y'know."

"I know," he says, "Lame."

"White people."

"Yeah, white people," he'd confirm. And then this is where things would get light.

"Come here often? What's your sign?" I'd say, and we'd laugh.

"You're one of the news reporters on Channel 7, right?"

"You recognize me? I haven't done many stories yet. Too young."

"But, you could be older, much older. Who knows with Asians? You could be, like, 87 for all they know. It's how we infiltrate."

"Asian invasion." We'd say this at the same time and laugh,

strangers sharing an inside joke. Already. At this moment, Chin—a complete stranger—would understand me more than my best girlfriends Tiff and Vickie.

Then, I could sigh, relax. Finally. Because Chin's not going to tell me, surprised, that I speak English so well. He's not going to tell me about how my people are, how Asians are good people, that he once knew a Chinese guy who was the hardest worker he ever knew—quiet, but a damned hard worker. And Chin would know the secrets: Most Asians are lactose intolerant, and many don't need to wear deodorant. He would know I've never eaten dogs and won't blame my bad driving on my race but my general anxiety. He wouldn't assume I'm really, really good at math—I suck at math. And he would know how it feels to be accused of being Asian.

And tonight I'd be the one going home with the nice guy while Tiff and Vickie are stuck with T-Shirt Man and Footloose. I imagine I leave SEEN with Chin, get in his BMW, and talk my yellow head off. We laugh easily, but I keep wanting to cry. It's just that I'm so comfortable. I tell him my parents are white and that I'm adopted and that I only knew two other Asian people in my life, besides the family across the street who owned The Golden Dragon restaurant, and whose house always smelled like fish sauce. You could smell it all the way from the sidewalk, I tell him, and he laughs because he knows what I'm talking about. We stop at Lafayette Coney Island for some chilidogs and fries and talk about his travels to South America, his love of Rock & Rye Faygo and Vernors, about how we both love Steinbeck, and how the film rendition of *Fight Club* is the best book-to-film translation of our time, even though we hated the book. Then, we hop back in his car and drive around for a couple of hours listening to Nina Simone and talking about our families before we go back to his place where he shakes up some martinis and we talk about getting the hell out of Michigan.

But my encounter with Chin doesn't happen like that.

It all happens the way I've told it—until the part when it's my turn to introduce myself. So, really, it goes like this: He says, "I'm Eddie Chin," and I say, "Abby Miller." We shake hands, and I promptly excuse myself to the bathroom, but really to get another drink.

I'm ashamed of myself. I know I should go back, try again, give this guy a chance. Perhaps give myself another chance. I know I'm skipping out on him just because he's Asian. Here's the thing. Two Asian people together = two immigrants = two dog munchers. It's like some weird rule. One Asian person alone can remain an anybody, personhood intact, racial features semi-invisible. Two or more Asians gathered in one spot and all of the sudden you become the Empire, moving in swiftly as an entire nation, all slanty eyes, flat-faces, math and pianos. Alone, I'm Abby. With Chin, I'm all of Asia and all of Asia's racial baggage. But, after all the classes in Asian-American literature, oppression theory, history of identity politics, I should know better. I do know better. I feel like a fraud.

I'm standing at the edge of the dance floor, watching Vickie get down Britney Spears style (post-Justin, pre-K-Fed) with T-shirt Man, who gropes her ass while she slinks around him as if he's a stripper pole. I watch from the bar with a fresh vodka tonic, a little embarrassed for her. Vickie sees me and waves. Then, T-shirt Man dances his way over to me. His head rocks back and forth on his thick neck, his hips sway from side to side, and his ass juts out every other beat as he walks—he's trying to dance toward me, but looks like he's trying to shake a fart out of his pants—and every once in a while, he closes his eyes to make a show of how much he's into the music.

"Whatcha drinkin'?" he asks.

"Water."

"Really," he says. "What are you drinking?"

"Water," I say. "Really."

"Y'know, Chin's over there." He points, but I don't look. I expect Chin's in exactly the same place I left him. Now, the problem is, I actually want to go over and talk to Chin because he is handsome, and I feel like a jerk, but I don't want to give any of these people the satisfaction of thinking that the only two Asian people in the room belong together because they are Asian.

"You should go talk to him," he says.

"You're his friend. You go talk to him."

"You're one of those banana girls, aren't you?" he says, meaning, yellow on the outside, white on the inside.

"Not cool," I say.

"Oh, sorry. A Twinkie, then?" He thinks he's pretty funny, like he's allowed to say these things to me because he probably says them to Chin, like he's an insider because his friend is Asian. He thinks if you get permission from one of us, you get permission from all of us. It's like the white kid who thinks he can say "nigger" because he hangs out with black kids, and the black kids don't mind because they are particular, specific black kids who just happen not to mind. But when that same white kid says "nigger" to another, different and particular, specific group of black kids, he gets his sorry ass beat. As such, I want to beat T-Shirt Man's ass.

"Don't worry," he says, "I'm not hitting on you. I'm into your friend, Vi ... Valerie. Really, I just thought you and Chin might hit it off."

"Why? Because we're Asian?"

"Why not?" He is sweating profusely, and I imagine the drops running down his forehead to be thick and sticky with hair gel.

The air in SEEN is steamy from all the drunken, sweaty bodies pushed together, dancing like they are on MTV, like they think they're the back-up dancers in a club scene for some Snoop Dog video. A draft of cool air blows in every once in a while as groups of people come and go.

Tiff and Chin are talking at a booth next to the bar. Vickie is on the dance floor thinking she's the hottest thing out there because she is. Granted she is the weather girl, plus she spent all of her high school years in an east coast conservatory studying dance. Other girls can't compete with her skills. That's why I stand against the bar. Or, that's one reason I stand against the bar. The other reason is for balance. I haven't been this drunk in years. I pick up my drink, and it tastes like vanilla, which means it is not my drink. In fact, I suddenly remember I finished my last vodka tonic a few minutes ago before going to the bathroom. But this drink tastes good. I decide the vanilla drink is my new favorite drink, and I take it with me over to a round table at the edge of the dance floor where T-Shirt Man sits, watching Vickie dance.

"Hey, T-Shirt Man," I say. The music is loud. "Hey!" It takes a minute for him to respond. He holds his index finger in the air, signaling to me I'll have to wait a sec because he's still watching my friend shake her ass like Shakira.

"T-Shirt Man, my man," I say. I put my hand in the air; I want him to give me a high-five.

"Chin's over there." He grabs my shoulders, spins me around on the vinyl seat, pointing me back toward the bar. "See him?" He raises his eyebrows as if I might score and shoos me away.

I know where Chin is. That's the problem. I've known where he's been all night and for the last half of the night, I've watched him schmooze with my best friend. What the hell? Why doesn't he want to get to know me? I'm the one who'd understand him. Tiff shouldn't even be talking to him. She's seeing two other guys right now, and both of them think it's exclusive. Chin should know better than to trust a girl like that. Doesn't he see how she's dressed, like a hooker? I must talk to Chin. This has gone too far. I stride over to where they're huddled.

"Excuse me," I say to Tiff. "Chin and I need to talk now."

"Is everything okay?" she says, acting innocent, like a woman who doesn't have two boyfriends, but I don't change my position.

"Now," I say. Tiff gets up with a huff and pushes past where I stand at the edge of the table.

"Chin," I say, "You're an Asian guy, right? So why don't you date Asian chicks?" I take a swig of the vanilla drink.

"Are you okay?"

"Answer my question, Chin."

"I think you should put your drink down for a moment."

"It's not my drink, Chin." I know I've stumped him. And now he's got to move on to my questions. "No more diversions, Chin. Get your own drink. Why don't you date Asian chicks?"

"Are you kidding?"

I bend forward and look him dead in the eye, slap my palm on the table. "Hey, Dog-Muncher," I say. "I'm the one asking questions here. I'm the reporter. Are you going to answer me or what, Chin?"

"No, I'm not. What is this about?"

"Hey, Chin. Do you care that people call you Chin, Chin? Doesn't it make you feel so Asian, Chin? Doesn't it? How does it feel to you, to be Asian, Chin?"

A familiar sadness opens on his face. Our eyes meet for a second, just long enough to acknowledge an unspoken code. Then, he gets up from the booth and sits me down in it. His arms are strong and confident. He pushes his glass of water toward me, and I take a long drink. Right now, all I want is to be home in my own bed with my dog curled at my feet.

"Chin, I love Misser Bitsy Baby," I slur.

He gives me a strange look and says, "Take another sip." He pushes the glass of water closer to me. I push it away, afraid I'll throw up. I slump into the booth, my head too heavy to hold so high. I try to apologize to Chin, but I can't seem to peel my face from the cool surface of the table. He pats my shoulder. "Good luck, Abby," he says, and when I try to signal for him to sit down, he's already gone, disappeared into the throng on the dance floor, the anonymous bodies moving like a singular entity. They rise and fall, showered in the spectacle of red and green and yellow lights, and if I could, I would heave myself out of the booth and, too, slip into the crowd, lose myself in the pulse of the night.

BETH KAUFKA was born in Seoul, South Korea but grew up in the Detroit area from infancy. She now lives with her husband and two daughters in Portland, Oregon where she teaches reading and writing in the Developmental Education program at Portland Community College. She is interested in all things pertaining to the empowerment and well-being of oppressed power-minority groups. Her work has been in *The Portland Review*, *Mid-American Review*, *Poets & Writers*, *Colorado Review*, *971 Menu*, *Kartika*, *WomenArts Quarterly* (forthcoming), and other academic journals. She is a 2007 winner of the AWP Intro Journals Award.

Masculinity and the
Asian American Male
by Byron Wong

I've been reading and writing about Asian American issues
since the early years of the internet. Before the internet, there
were few outlets for Asian American public discourse—no
national Asian American magazines that focused on serious
issues, no investigative TV programs, and no public forums.
Everything changed with the internet. No longer were people
constrained by geography or access to other Asian people—
anyone with a computer connection could post an opinion
or article on Asian American issues or read what others were
saying. The early internet message boards with sites such as
asianguy.com, goldsea.com, yellowworld.org, modelminority.
com, and thefighting44s.com allowed Asian Americans to
converse freely on any topic. One might expect an explosion
of diverse topics related to the Asian American experience, but
left to the dictates of the crowd, every message board seemed
to revert back to a common topic: interracial relationships.
Forums were filled with angry Asian men asking why Asian
women preferred to date White men over Asian men. Most
had comment policies on discussing the issue—some would
moderate to ensure the discussion didn't become overheated;
some restricted discussion of the IR (Interracial Relationship)
disparity to certain threads or areas of the website, while others
allowed a general free-for-all. But the end effect was more or
less the same: the forums would erupt into contentious gender
wars over interracial relationships.

Most students of Asian America don't find this singular focus surprising—at some point in our lives, the IR question has
affected us all. It's hard to face rejection because of one's race,

especially from the women of one's race, and for many Asian American men, it appears to be a major disturbance in their lives. These days, it's rare to find an Asian American female celebrity who is married to another Asian American male; most are married to White men. The IR disparity has been an issue in America for a long time. In the early 1970s, Frank Chin wrote:

> The Japanese American Citizens League (JACL) weekly, the *Pacific Citizen*, in February, 1972, reported that more than 50% of Japanese American women were marrying outside their race and that the figure was rising annually. Available statistics indicate a similar trend among Chinese American women, though the 50 percent mark may not have been topped yet. These figures say something about our sensibility, our concept of Chinese America and Japanese America, our self-esteem, as does our partly real and partly mythical silence in American culture.[1]

Most men say that the disparity arises because Asian women have a significant preference for White men. Most Asian women agree, but there are also women who argue that the disparity arises because Asian men aren't aggressive enough in pursuing Asian women. Both statements are true—experts and social scientists have conducted studies that indicate the existence of a White preference among Asian women,[2] and anecdotal evidence seems to indicate a lack of aggressiveness among Asian men in dating.[3] After years of discussing the issue online, a significant number of Asian men have begun to seek solutions by focusing on the causes—what makes Asian women prefer White men, and what makes Asian men less aggressive? Many Asian American male commenters on my website have come to the conclusion that the root of the problem lies in manliness or masculinity. They argue that White men act more masculine, whether as a group or as individuals, and that this masculinity gives White men an advantage in the dating game—both in terms of attracting Asian women and in being more aggressive with Asian women. Nearly everyone acknowledges that the social and institutional power that White men hold in American society also plays a significant role. Many Asian American men want solutions that will change this skewed dynamic. They would like to be on equal footing in the dating and marriage match-ups. They want to be seen as the worthy people they are. The internet discussions that take place on Asian American message boards are attempts to intellectually find this worthiness.

One of my blog commenters, a Korean American man who goes by the name "kobukson," posed the question of how we defined masculinity. He wrote:

I realize using the word itself can push a few psychic buttons in the Asian-American male psyche. Because the rallying cry in the oppressed Asian American male ethnic studies department is "emasculation." Emasculation means that your balls have been cut off. By whom? The official dogma states that it is the evil conspiracy of Hollywood, the white male power structure, and Asian women.

I propose that much of this emasculation originates within our own families, communities, and is even self-inflicted.[4]

Kobukson places the blame on Asian American men, referencing our families and communities and calling the problem self-inflicted. What followed under my blog post was a long, fascinating discussion on how we defined the term "masculinity." Through a diverse panel of commenters, we collectively came to the conclusion that masculinity, as most of us define it, is simply aggressive *yang* action, intelligent or not. I wrote: "To be masculine is to embody brave and aggressive action towards the fulfillment of one's explicit main goals."[5]

We created a different blog discussion to help define "manliness," and a majority of us came to the conclusion that manliness was a function of what one's culture expected from men. Masculinity, therefore, was power and aggressiveness irrespective of culture, while manliness came from a culture's value system of what men should be. Masculinity was a descriptor, while manliness was a code. But what I found even more interesting was that masculinity, according to our discussions, had little to do with what women desired in a man, but rather what men desired in themselves. For Asian men, the discussion was especially enlightening—within the internet discussions, Asian men often spent so much time discussing the damage from the interracial relationship disparity that we neglected to focus on who we are as men, independent of what women want men to be.

In other words, the IR disparity is both a symptom and a cause of other problems in our culture. Past statements are correct—the IR disparity exists, and it perpetuates a racial hierarchy. It creates disadvantages for Asian men, and we ought to work to reverse the imbalance. But it's not the only issue on the table, and it may not even be the most significant issue on the table. If we remove Asian women from the equation and focus on masculinity, Asian men still have problems. We may not be what many Asian women want, but more importantly, we aren't what we want. And when we confront the disparity, irrespective of the question of whether or not it's wrong or right, our fights are solitary rather than social or communal, and we spend most of our efforts fighting internal demons from our past rather than external problems in our present.

The silent sufferer is the quintessential stereotype of the Asian American male—the quiet studious nerd who is inept at talking to women and who plays video games for fun. White boys embody the "masculine" stereotypes by playing sports and speaking loudly, moving objects through the air, focusing on physical force, playing team sports rather than engaging in solitary endeavors. Asian boys ponder academic math problems or engage in rote memorization, while White boys engage in creative pursuits—rock music, football, and thinking of creative ways to interact with girls.

Thus arise the stereotypes of Asian men vs. White men in feminine vs. masculine pursuits. Men are supposed to be primarily focused on external concerns—moving objects through space, creating energy by organizing fellow men into teams, and conquering other people whether on the battlefield, the sports field, or the boardroom. Dealing with emotional issues, at least according to the stereotype, is supposed to be the primary domain of women. Even when history looks at men who embody both masculine power and feminine introspection, society evaluates them primarily on their masculine traits. Abraham Lincoln may have struggled with emotional depression, but winning the Civil War and emancipating the slaves overshadow all of his internal battles. The softer and darker side of Abraham Lincoln is almost a footnote in his popular image as war president and liberator.

We Asian men have lost our masculinity and manliness. Another commenter on my blog, ChineseMom, is a Chinese American woman with pre-teen children who immigrated after attending a top university in China. ChineseMom says that manliness is similar in Western and Chinese societies—people admire honor, loyalty, and speaking from the gut in men—but Western society emphasizes it more. She attributes this partly to the explosion of capitalism in relatively poor China. "Act like a man," according to ChineseMom, means the same thing in both countries, but it means less in a country where people are more worried about making money and surviving. Ultimately our values are similar in terms of how we measure men.

The counterargument is that Americans and Chinese seem to view men's behaviors differently. Holding a woman's purse and having Hello Kitty trinkets on one's cell phone are examples of behaviors that might damage a man's reputation in the U.S. but not in China. ChineseMom also brought up the example of Gou Jian, a king of Yue in ancient China who ate the king of Wu's feces in order to ride the storm before defeating Wu. Such an action would likely cause an American man irreparable harm, while the Chinese lionization of Gou Jian might seem to indicate a Chinese respect for the kind of intelligence and fortitude to endure pain while waiting for opportunity.

We don't know if we can completely resolve the IR disparity. We've identified two causes, and the "attraction" cause may well be beyond our control—some Asian women may prefer White men no matter what we do. At the same time, there seems to be a clear path for Asian American men to become *more* successful in our interactions with the opposite sex and in our quest to earn respect as men, not just from women but from other men. We need to become more masculine—to employ brave and aggressive action in our lives with less hesitation. No more simply staring at women—we need to approach them. No more simply working for the Man—we need to push for advancement or run our own businesses. No more simply accepting society's rules as they are—if the rules are not right, we need to empower ourselves to change them. No more sitting on the sidelines—we need to get involved. If we take strong action, we can guarantee better results, both in terms of the IR disparity and our masculinity issues. Every small piece of improvement is a step in the right direction.

This mantra of "take action" has been a part of the common prescription among Asian American activists for a long time. Activists often speak about the APAthetic APA (Asian Pacific American) community, telling the community that they must mobilize in order to actualize, focusing specifically on Asian American men. More and more Asian American men are in fact joining causes, and we're beginning to notice more Asian men in the news media who are taking action to better their communities and to make their voices heard—the staggering number of elected politicians in California is a prime example of how people in our community are standing up. Masculinity among Asian men clearly already exists. But has it filtered down to the rest of society outside of our superstars?

Looking at the IR disparity and the words and complaints that Asian women make about Asian American men today, the answer most likely is still no. Why don't we stand up more? Why don't we "man up?" It seems simple, but it's not. Most people *can't* stand up perfectly and immediately after sitting for years.

In the Canadian TV series *Being Erica*, the main character Erica, after a string of romances with traditionally manly men, falls in love with a character named Adam, a man in her therapy group who struggles with internal issues stemming from a physically and mentally abusive childhood. Adam makes enough money to live on his own. He has a job where his boss likes his work, and he lives in a rich city where there are social services and plenty of resources. Adam has everything he needs to succeed. Yet he finds himself fighting against his tendencies at every turn, taking on a passive aggressive attitude with Erica, holding back information from his therapist, and struggling with a self-imposed inability to take action. To paraphrase kobukson's indictment of the Asian American community, Adam's emasculation originates from his own family and community and is self-inflicted. Even though his family and community no longer play a significant role in his life, Adam still carries the injuries.

Asian men are in a similar situation. Look at the outpouring of emotion following Amy Chua's publication of *Battle Hymn of the Tiger Mother*, and it's clear that many of us carry emasculating injuries from our upbringings. Most of us never played childhood games that encouraged fast verbal fluency, and many of us may come from families that discouraged self-expression. We're similar to the character Adam—there are no visible barriers in front of us, but there still exist barriers in our own minds that others cannot see.

So what is the solution? How do we stop being a culture of undeveloped men? How do we become more masculine?

First, there's nothing wrong with being undeveloped as long as we're making progress. If we think of life as a journey, everyone begins at one point and ends at another point while crossing many other points in between. We all have our obstacles to conquer, and whether these obstacles are internal or external does not detract from the heroism of the person fighting against them. It takes courage, intelligence, and power to fight a legacy of physical and mental abuse, abandonment, and toxic parenting. It takes bold action to fight against one's cultural pathologies. People need to recognize the struggle of Asian American men. As dark and as atypically masculine as Asian American men's internal battles may be, we deserve respect for the difficulty of the struggle.

At the same time, there exists a unique honor in having the skills, means, and confidence to use one's mind and body to change or improve the outside world. We need masculine men, men who are not afraid of stepping up to external challenges and winning the fights they take on. We have men in our community who are naturally inclined towards alpha-maleness, and there are already powerful Asian American men who have made great achievements in society. But we need to enable more such men to succeed, and we need to raise more such men in our communities. To do so, we need to create an environment that encourages men to challenge themselves.

There have been blog posts and books written on the topic of "alpha Asian" men and how men can become stronger, and most of these blog posts are right—there are many areas where we can improve our families and communities to encourage Asian men to find their external strengths. Many of the problems that Asian men face are similar to problems all men face, with small adjustments for cultural differences, and many of the solutions to these problems work against both internal and external battles. My favorite book on teaching men to reclaim power is *The Wonder of Boys* by Michael Gurian. Here are some ideas from his book, adapted for Asian Americans:

Asian men need honor. In these modern times, men often focus their attention on computer screens and passive entertainment. We need to actively learn to be truthful and good in our actions and words.

Asian men need structure. Following the 1960s when Americans challenged traditional values and beliefs, we stopped believing in structure within society. Men need to know that the world makes sense and that we can succeed by living our principles.

Asian men need rituals. Books on manhood often address male rituals and how our ancestors learned manhood through a well-defined path. These are great ideas that Asian American men ought to examine. We need new ways to teach Asian American boys to become men.

Asian men need to learn how to take risks. High payouts in life come from making decisions that involve educated risks, whether we're discussing throwing a football to a teammate, investing in a business, or trying to make a new friend. Men need to learn confidence in their ability to take intelligent risks.

Asian men need a journey. We all need goals, and we all need society's support in achieving them. Men themselves, when they are of the age when they can make good decisions, need to choose a journey on their own.

These are some concrete steps that Asian men can take to create masculinity in themselves and in their sons. This is an area where we can make structural changes to refocus our goals and outlook to bring about a more powerful form of masculinity. These changes are independent of culture. They are universal journeys that men of all cultures have traditionally sought. Somehow in the process of assimilation, Asian American men lost these goals. If we can refocus our energy on recreating these goals, we can reclaim our lost masculinity.

My blog traffic has steadily increased over the years, with the biggest spikes in traffic coming from the same familiar topics of all Asian American blogs: interracial dating and masculinity. Sometimes when I'm bored, in the middle of my normal posts about news, philosophy, and literature, I'll throw in an interracial dating or masculinity article just to get comments flooding in. After ten years of discussion in the blogosphere, the topic continues to generate pages and pages of discussion. Many of my commenters will counsel others by saying that the situation will not change, that the best course of action is to move on from the destruction that the IR disparity and emasculation have caused. "Just ignore it and try to date White women" is a frequent piece of advice that readers offer to one another. While I agree with the sentiment of "moving on," I take a holistic view of the situation. In his book *Light on Life*, B.K.S. Iyengar says that "Duality is the seed of conflict," and that yogic tradition says that freedom only comes with "Oneness."[6] I tend to agree with this. Like any disparity, the interracial dating disparity and masculinity disparity create disharmony and imbalance. It's hard to feel the happiness of "oneness" when we feel the sting of discrimination or inequality.

People talk about these topics because they want to understand them and to improve their lives. They want to restore harmony and balance in both their lives and their culture. Asian men want to date Asian women, and I believe that most Asian women, regardless of which race they prefer as marriage partners, find troubling the unbalanced preference that Asian women give to White men in this country. In the end, our best course of action is to improve a little at a time by finding ways to stretch ourselves to new levels of masculinity and to focus our energy on closing the interracial dating disparity. Men need goals and structure, and we need to learn to be expressive. For Asian American men, we can build power, aggressiveness, and self-knowledge in a manner that can help us find peace and acceptance with Asian women and also with ourselves. Rather than having a gender war on internet forums, perhaps someday we can have gender unity, along with unity in Asian American masculinity. Freedom exists in *oneness*.

NOTES

[1] Frank Chin, et al., *Aiiieeeee! An Anthology of Asian American Writers* (New York, NY: Penguin Books, 1991) preface, xii-xiii.

[2] See John Tierney's blog post "Single Female Seeking Same Race Male": "For equal success with an Asian woman, an African-American needs no additional income; a white man needs $24,000 less than average; a Hispanic man needs $28,000 more than average." http://tierneylab.blogs.nytimes.com/2007/04/13/single-female-seeking-same-race-male/

Or see Steve Penner's article "Racial Preferences in the Dating World": "The one major exception to the finding that women wanted to meet men of their own race was Asian women, a vast majority of whom stated that they strongly preferred meeting non-Asian men. The primary explanation offered by most Asian women was that they wanted to be matched with tall men, and they insisted that practically all of the Asian men they knew were short. But when I would ask if they would be willing to meet an Asian man if he were tall, most would simply shake their head and say they would rather not." http://www.seacoastonline.com/apps/pbcs.dll/article?AID=/20070511/OPINION04/70511017/-1/OPINION05

[3] This is mostly anecdotal, but see this humorous video: http://www.youtube.com/watch?v=rTASOI8SVjU&feature=player_embedded

[4] kobukson [pseud], comment on "I'll Keep You My Dirty Little Secret, Dirty Little Secret, Dirty Little Secret ... ," bigwowo.com, entry February 17, 2011, comment posted February 23, 2011, http://www.bigwowo.com/2011/02/ill-keep-you-my-dirty-little-secret-dirty-little-secret-dirty-little-secret/#comment-9480 [accessed October 10, 2011]
http://www.bigwowo.com/2011/02/asian-american-masculinity/

[5] Special thanks to my commenters "kobukson," "nottyboy," "urB4N," "Chinese Mom," and "King" for their contributions and inputs.

[6] B.K.S. Iyengar, *Light on Life* (USA: Rodale, 2005), 16

BYRON WONG is a mortgage banker in Portland, Oregon. He helped co-found Thymos in 2004. He blogs and podcasts at bigWOWO.com and is a former blogger at thefighting44s.com.

Significant Moments
in the Life of Oriental Faddah and Son
by Lee A. Tonouchi

Significant Moments in the Life
of Oriental Faddah and Son:
BIRTH

I would like fo' tink
he started off wit one
yosh.

Or, if he wuz feeling
particularly peppy
maybe one unbridled,
one unrestrained
YOOOOOOOOOOOOOOSH
for demonstrate
his virility.

Cuz I know
my Oriental Faddah,
he not one man
of many words,
of much emotion.
He probably made due wit
grunt.

Jus one grunt
fo' send da message
dat he done,
through,

all pau,
time fo' go sleep now.

Das all I can imagine
my Oriental Faddah
saying wen him and my Ma
wuz trying for conceive me.

He jus not da type fo' say
"Oh yeah,
work it, baby, work it.
C'mon down,
let's get funky
like a monkey."

Nope.
Grunt.
Jus one.

Significant Moments in the Life of Oriental Faddah and Son: PUBERTY

For my 13th birthday
my Oriental Faddah
gave me my long awaited
Cosby Show talk
about da birds
and da bees.

I know if Da Cos
did 'em
would probably take
forevah and a day
cuz wenevah Da Cos talks

ees always
so drawn out:

"Son, a long time agooooooo
the birds and the beeeeeeeees
hooked up. So that is whyyyyyy
The stork
took over
for them . . . "

I know my Oriental Faddah
could nevah
sustain one speech
fo' dat long.
So I wuz anticipating
someting li'lo bit mo' concise,
but not someting dat would take
only 2.2 seconds.

Cuz all he did wuz hand me
one black T&C T-shirt
wit one smiley face
balloon character
and fluorescent
yellow lettahs dat sed
"No Glove,
No Love."

Das it,
no explainations.
Not even one hint
dat we wuz talking
metaphor.

Significant Moments in the Life
of Oriental Faddah and Son:
COLLEGE

Aftah I wen graduate high school
my Oriental Faddah
wanted me for go
Harvard, Princeton, Stanford,
AND Yale.

He nevah know
wea any of those places wuz,
jus dat das wea I had fo' go.
So I went
UC Irvine.

Das wea I wen discover
dat my Oriental Faddah
wuzn't really
my Oriental Faddah.

He wuz my
"Asian American" Faddah.

Dey sed I can have one Oriental rug
or some Oriental furnitures,
but I cannot
CAN
NOT
have
one Oriental Faddah.

Oriental is one term you use
for da kine inanimate objecks.
Ass wot dey toll me.

So, I toll 'em,
"Oh, my Oriental Faddah,
he hardly sez anyting.
Das kinda like
being one inanimate objeck, ah.
Wotchoo tink?"

Ho, wen I sed dat
their faces wen jus
freeeeeze,
like dey couldn't believe
I sed someting
as disrespeckful as dat.

Tsk, "Asian American" ass why.

Significant Moments in the Life of Oriental Faddah and Son: MARRIAGE

I came back home
wit one girlfriend
fiancé actually
who wuz one katonk.

Only she nevah know she wuz
one katonk.
She probably mo' used to
da term
banana.

Either way, my Oriental Faddah
wuz happy
katonk, banana,
TWINKIE,
so long as Oriental he sed,

"Asian American," she correck-ed.

Jus for fun
I took her to one
Frank Delima show
at da Polynesian Palace.

But she nevah laugh,
not even one chuckle
for wot she called
"the blatant
stereotyping
and racist
ethnic portrayals."

So I started playing around, brah.
Aftah da show,
I started telling all my friends

"Eh, wassup Oriental!"

"Ooo, you frickin' Oriental!"

"Brah, yo' mama, she so Oriental
I bet she cannot see her chopsticks
unless she turn 'em sideways!"

I figgah I would take back
da term!

If Popolo people can
use da "N" word, den hakum
I cannot use da one
dat starts wit "O?"

EMPOWERING li'dat.

She tot I wuz nuts.
Out of my freakin' mind!

So she got back on her plane
and leff.

Looking in da air
all I could tink wuz
Wot Lucille,
You going leave me now?!

Even though Lucille
wuzn't even
her name.

Significant Moments in the Life of Oriental Faddah and Son: DEATH

Right befo'
my Oriental Faddah died
he suddenly had
planny fo' say.

"No watch Kingpin,
da movie juuunk.
The English Patient
mo' bettah wuz, but
not as good as
da book."

Ho, dat shocked da hell outta me
cuz I nevah know he went movies,
let alone read books.

I tot he jus stayed home
watched Abarenbo Shogun
on KIKU
and drank da kine green tea, li'dat.

But now he wuz giving me
da lowdown
on all da latest movies.

I toll 'em, Haw
I could jus picture him
on TV, brah.
At The Movies
wit Roger Ebert
and my Oriental Faddah.
And people would ax
"Oh, which one is Ebert?"
DUH, da one das not Oriental!

He laughed little bit
den he coughed
and axed
real soft
if I tot people
would really mix up
him
and Roger Ebert.

I toll 'em
Nah,
Roger Ebert
get glasses.

Das wot I toll
to
my Faddah.

Obaban's Hands

by Lee A. Tonouchi

I nevah like get
da kine generic
kanji character,
dat kine most guys get
on da back
of their shoulder blades,
"chikara"
fo' show dey strong,
tough,
cuz one tattoo tells one story —
"Oh, I got chikara
cuz I tink I have muscles"
is kinda one junk story.

My friend Jay
agreed dat cliché kine is junk.
Das da reason why
he nevah like get
one crane, tiger, or dragon.
He sed, Asian American males
are always typecast as being
masters of da martial arts.
So for challenge dat notion
he got one peace symbol instead,
not da Chinese calligraphy kine, but
y'know dat upsidedown airplane in da circle,
which wuz pretty ironic to me
cuz Jay had
one black belt
in Tae Kwon Do

and he liked
getting into fights
and beating people up,
so I figgah-ed advertising
he wanted for beef
would be good, no?

My oddah friend Rayceen,
she cannot even handle
peeling da band-aid off her leg
so we wuz surprised
wen she got one sexy
geisha girl
on her lower back
as some kine "feminist statement"
against da stereotype
of da "submissive Asian female."
Someting li'dat she sed.
Wuz one interesting idea,
I tot to myself,
but wouldn't dat only work
if you wuz one loudmout tita girl.
Oddahwise guys going tink
you same same like da picture.
Plus not like those chopsticks
in your hair helps.

For explore my
various tattoo possibilities
I called up my Grandma and axed her
if we had one family crest
and if so
wot da ting looked like?

My grandma laughed wen I axed her.
"Okinawa all farmer, y'know?
Fancy design, das Naichi style,

himakamaka.
We Uchinanchu. Dey used to
tease us befo' time.
We all da buta kaukau people,
da people who eat pig.
To us, ono was. We like pig,
but to dem
pig feet soup
low class food dat was."

I wuz tinking about if
anybody in our family had
any tattoos
and das wen I remembered
Obaban.

Wen I wuz small I wuz sked
for let Obaban
touch me cuz I thought
she had one disease
or someting cuz
da back of her hands
wuz all tattooed,
colored with shapes
of solid black,
like square bruises.

I axed my Grandma
if she knew da meanings for dat.
She sed in ancient times
da Uchinanchu high priestess
wuz returning home to Okinawa,
but her boat got lost
in one typhoon
so she ended up in Japan.
Da Japanese lord dude
thought she wuz one hottie

so he kept her prisoner, li'dat.
But da high priestess
wuzn't all looks and no brains.
Witout his knowing
she wen go tattoo
da back of her hands,
so he wouldn't tink
she wuz so pretty anymore.
Wen da lord dude saw wot she did
he wen freak,
like wot da fuck is dat,
so he sent her back home.
And from dat point on,
all da women in Okinawa
started doing 'em
for ward off all da Japanese pirates.
At least das how da legend goes.

Dis made me retink
my whole tattoo theories.
If Okinawa farmer people style is
make yourself look unattractive
as possible den I no like pay money
for make myself look ugly!

Das wen I got da perfeck idea.
Wen people ax if I evah thought about
getting one tattoo,
I can tell 'em,
Oh, in Okinawa
wuz traditionally
da women who got tattoo-ed
and from dea I can buss out
da whole pirate deals.
Bu-ya. Save money
and
I get one story for tell.

Kalihi Valley Girl

by Lee A. Tonouchi

I'm only telling you this because I'm like nice and all and you're the new girl here. Maybe this is your first time going to a private school, yeah, but if I were you, what I'd ask for this Christmas is like, a full makeover. That's really what you need, no? I mean take a look at you, like seriously. The way you look, the way you talk, the way you feel—it all sends out a message. And the message I'm getting from you is a desperate cry for help.

Okay, for starters take your top. What does it say on your shirt? I like see. Ainokea? Like, what is that? I ... No ... Care. Isn't that Pidgin? I can't believe people in Hawai'i still talk Pidgin. Pidgin sounds so stu-pid. Ainokea? Isn't that like that dumb moke brand? You like the slogan? "Ainokea, I Do What I Like." You like it because you think it's saying you should feel free to be who you wanna be no matter what people say? Au contraire. Maybe I'm like too literal, cause that's not what it's saying to me. Sounds like it's saying everyone shouldn't care. Like you're saying you want total chaos. Judging you from your hair, maybe you do. I don't get it. Why are you announcing to the world that you're apathetic and that you don't care? You should stand for something. You should care. Everybody knows that, no? Like hello.

And I don't know if you do it, but you probably do do it because all you, what's the word, tee-ta, all you tee-tas do it. You should avoid being all in your face and using uppity language like, "Ho brah, what, eye problems?!" and "Ho sistah, watch it!" There's always classier ways to express yourself without resorting to the use of "Ho." How many times do you hear H-town celebrities dropping the H-bomb? Well Kathy Griffin drops F-bombs, which I suppose is worse than the H-bomb. But as everyone knows, Kathy Griffin is a D-list celebrity. For the A-listers, whom we all aspire to be like, if they can do it, we can do it too. For example, instead of saying "Ho cuz" to express your displeasure. You should get into the habit of saying something more educated and sophisticated like, "That's way harsh" or "What-ever."

I don't know what we're gonna do with you. You just have a look that's better suited for radio. Like, do you even work out? You go swimming at the beach with your parents and your cousins? Not even. That's so ten years ago. Why would you want to be seen with your family? You need to get out, to be seen by people who like ... matter. You need to get like a spa membership or something. I like it when people see me in my cute workout outfits, but that's because I'm pretty and people like looking at pretty people. See. So I'm just giving people what they want.

For you, do you even open the light when you pick out clothes from your closet? My clothes are chic. Your clothes reek. No, I don't mean they stink. Maybe you're the literal one. Do you even think about what brands you wear? Where do you do your shopping? That's what I like know. Goodwill? Like, oh, my God. Not even. You do? Are you homeless? My bad. I don't want to be like a snob and half, but if you like fit in here, you should remember this advice. Thrift stores ... don't go there. Duh.

And what's going on here? What are you holding? That's a big fashion faux pas. You need to get yourself a purse. That is not a purse. That's a wallet. You just carry around your wallet like that? You have to put your wallet in something. And the correct answer isn't your backpack or your pocket. You need a nice satchel or a hobo bag. And you might've gotten some snaps for your ripper wallet back in elementary school, but this is high school. You need to lose the velcro and invest in something leather. Do you even read fashion magazines? *Glamour? Lucky? Cosmo?* No idea? Not a clue have you?

Is there anyone here at our school who might you consider to be your fashion icon? Gimme a hint? What alphabet does her name start with? Okay, that wasn't the letter I was like expecting. Unless you think my name has a silent W. So which alphabet? E?

E is okay. Are you thinking of Erica? Ewwww. Flared jeans and teased hair were so last season. That girl should like keep up, no? If you want people to like you, you should fully take notes on how Shanna and Nikki dress. They're models you know. But they cheat a little because they have good genetics. They're tall because their dad's Haole. They don't need five inch heels like you. No, you can't wear five inch slippers. What are you? FOB?

Since you don't seem to know anything about stores, lemme make it simple for you. If you're really unsure about whether or not a store's worthy, then you test it by seeing if Paris would go. What do you mean where? Paris is not a where. Paris is a who. Everyone knows celebrities who matter are all referred to by their first names only. What do you mean why is she a celebrity? She's famous for being famous. Like duh. The Paris shopping test is simple. It goes like this. You ask, Prada? The answer is, Paris would go. Gucci? Paris would go. See, so the next time you're considering buying clothes from Wal-Mart you put yourself in Paris' Jimmy Choo's and you ask Wal-Mart? And the answer is Paris would NOT go. In fact, Paris would be all like "Wal-Mart? Is that where they sell walls?"

Someday I wanna be like rich and have my own reality show and become a celebrity. I know, I know, it's quite an ambition. That's why my fallback plan is just to marry someone rich. If I can do that, then voila, the other pieces will fall into place. That's why appearances are important. It's for the career path I have chosen. I'm not vain. I'm not like Kim making a whole calendar with pictures of myself to show off my big booty. Because I don't think I'm superficial. I believe beauty all starts from the inside, no? Beauty all starts from within. That's why diet is important. Because if you put junk on your inside, you look junk on the outside. Simple as that.

Notice how I eat a lotta Lean Cuisine for my lunch. Generally, if what you're eating sounds foreign, then it at least gives the appearance that you're worldly. And you should make it a habit to say things like "The Fettuccini Alfredo is Esquisito" and "The Portabello Stuffed Rigatoni is tres fantastique." If I'm gonna make it in H-town, people can't know I'm from this rock. They have to think I'm cultured and cosmopolitan. This might be a little too advanced for you. You may wanna be like me, but not everyone can, okay? But you're welcome to try.

Take a look at what's in your package you got for lunch. What you got? The rule is if Jessica can't identify your can good, then you probably shouldn't eat it. I don't think Jessica would know what you got there. She'd be all like what is Spam? Is that fish or chicken? It's impossible to make Spam sound cultured. I'm sorry, but you can't fool anyone with Spam. No matter what you say. I'm glad you're sorta sticking to my rules. Nice try sounding international with your, "Dis Spam musubi is supa 'ONO." In theory that may be cosmopolitan, but rather than using Hawaiian you should stick to sprinkling Italian or French words into your vocabularies.

When all else fails, remember this ... words are like fine wines. All the good ones come from France and Italy. Even California wines are highly regarded. So that's why it's totally okay to say phrases like "waaay" and "fer shur." After all, you know what's in California, right? Like, yeah. Hollywood baby. And that's where I'm headed.

"Da Pidgin Guerrilla" LEE A. TONOUCHI is da writer of da award-winning book of Pidgin short stories *Da Word* (Bamboo Ridge, 2001), author of da Pidgin essay collection *Living Pidgin: Contemplations on Pidgin Culture* (Tinfish, 2002), compiler of *Da Kine Dictionary: Da Hawai'i Community Pidgin Dictionary Projeck* (Bess, 2005), and editor of *Buss Laugh: Stand Up Poetry from Hawai'i* (Bess, 2009). Da Honolulu Theatre for Youth wen do his play *Three Year Swim Club* (2010). An'den Kumu Kahua Theatre wen stage his plays *Gone Feeshing* (2004), *Living Pidgin* (2007), and *Da Kine Space* (2011).

Our Man Obama:
The Post-Imperial Presidency
by Andrew Lam

Having come from a country whose wretched history is largely defined by being colonized or fought over by the various empires, and being a reader of the modern novel, I see the rise of Barack Obama as the beginning of the end of a five-hundred-year-old colonial curse.

Decades ago, English still unruly on my tongue, I read a spin-off of Daniel Defoe's *Robinson Crusoe*, but not the way most of my American peers did. I, on one level or another, saw myself in Friday, Crusoe's servant.

A British sailor participating in the slave trade, Crusoe was shipwrecked off the coast of Venezuela. He was alone for some years but managed with his guns to rescue a native prisoner who was about to be eaten by his captors. He named him Man Friday, taught him English, and converted him to Christianity. He taught Friday to call him "master."

James Joyce once noted that Defoe's sailor is the symbol of the imperial conquest, that "he is the true prototype of the British colonist ... The whole Anglo-Saxon spirit is in Crusoe: the manly independence, the unconscious cruelty, the persistence, the slow yet efficient intelligence, the sexual apathy, the calculating taciturnity."

Likewise, all of those who have been colonized and oppressed in the age of European expansionism are embodied in Friday. Indentured and "saved" by Crusoe, Friday has become, over the centuries, a political symbol of racial injustice, of victims of colonization and imperialist expansion, of slavery. Friday was African, Native American, Asian, Latin American. And Friday was all the children born from miscegenation.

When he was christened, when he called Crusoe "master," Friday essentially lost his autonomy and his past. When he was taught a new language, Friday lost his bearings and the articulation and enchantment of his old tongue.

In the aftermath of the age of European conquest, many went in search of identity—cultural, national, personal—but the legacy remained largely that of an inferiority complex, a kind of grievance trap that was, for those previously subordinated by the West, nearly impossible to escape.

The power structure is stacked against them. Along with that sense of inferiority, their legacy is often disorganization and distrust. Even if no longer conquered, they remain vanquished—in a world redefined largely by the victors; their sense of value is fragmented, their sense of self unmoored. English is the global language of choice. From Western-style clothing to commerce to political dominance, history seems largely defined by the West. Species long known to natives are constantly "discovered" and given Latin and Greek names. Tall mountains are to be "summited" by wealthy westerners while the bent-backed Sherpas simply climb. Ancient settlements are destroyed, old temples are razed and the new structures built upon them are christened with the names of Catholic saints. Even the cosmos is crowded with Greek and Roman gods.

For a while, I grieved. Then I resigned myself to the idea that I was fated to live at the empire's outer edge, in a world in which Friday's children were destined to play subservient roles and act as sidekicks. I knew this because I saw it on TV nightly. Friday became Tonto, Mammy, Pocahontas, and Kato. I saw, too, the complexity of my own Vietnamese past ignored or, worse yet, simplified and reduced to faceless figures in black pajamas and conical hats, to serve as props or to be gunned down by American GIs, the wielders of history.

Defoe's narrative has become so deeply institutionalized that it continues to serve as the core premise of Western culture. Growing up as an outsider, the story I internalized was the supremacy of Crusoe's children. It wasn't a conscious narrative, perhaps, but it became in time a cynicism, and a given: no matter how well you perform and how smart you are, you are not to be in the center, in the place of real power.

Until a decade or so ago, when minorities began to play central roles in the movies, the theme of Crusoe's glory continued to play out unimpeded. *The Swiss Family Robinson* as well as *Robinson Crusoe on Mars* and dozens more movies were direct spin-offs, but the book's mythos also provided the backbone for TV shows like *Star Trek*, on which the captain is white and his crew are ethnic and aliens, and contemporary films like *Men in Black*, *Jerry Maguire*, *Pulp Fiction*, and *Lethal Weapon*, just to name very few. In them the ethnic sidekicks help make the main character who he is, reinforcing his character and centrality. With few exceptions, the white man leads, the minority characters follow—for such is the shape of the culture and the unwritten rule taught subliminally not so long ago, a curse of superior-inferior fiction that many ingested as fact.

Who knows, then, when the story began to shift?

Perhaps the resistant narratives were there all along, existing as scars on the slave's back, and in pockets in the various regions and with various subjugated peoples waiting to form a chorus, waiting for the right conductor to come along to form a new symphony.

It may very well have begun when the first slave, robbed of his freedom, his language, but not his music, sang his holy howls in the vast expanse of cotton fields, and in time it turned into the blues and gave birth to American music. In literature, it most gloriously began with Frederick Douglass. Lewis Hyde, in his seminal work *Trickster Makes This World*, regards Douglass as a kind of trickster—like Hermes or Loki or Eshu—who learned to reallocate power, a "cunning go-between ...[a] thief of reapportionment who quit the periphery and moved to the center."

Born a slave in Maryland in 1818 to white father and black mother, Douglass learned the alphabet from his master's wife. He stole books. He learned how to read and write. He taught others. He became an abolitionist, editor, suffragist, author, and the first African American nominated in the U.S. for vice president, in 1872 on the Equal Rights Party ticket with Victoria Woodhull, the first woman to run for president.

But what did Douglass steal, exactly? The language of the masters, of course; their eloquence. And he mastered it. He spoke up. He thereby crossed the color lines, the demarcations that he was not supposed to cross. He wrote autobiographies: *Narrative of the Life of Frederick Douglass, an American Slave; My Bondage and My Freedom*; and *The Life and Times of Frederick Douglass*—and, according to Hyde, his stories challenged and broke "the rule of silence" and "contest the white world's fiction about slavery," liberating him and, in turn, others.

For this is the way the power lies: those who once dwelled at the margins of the commonwealth have appropriated the language of their colonial masters, and they use it with a great degree of articulation as they inch toward the center, crossing all kinds of demarcations, dispelling the old myth. If Crusoe contends that he still is the lead actor, Friday is not content to play subservient and sidekick any longer.

That old superior-inferior fiction is further eroded by the way history flows. The America that received my family and me in the mid-seventies, for instance, was an America that could not possibly fathom the coming of a Pacific Century. The rise of the Far East, its cultural and economic influences lapping now at the American shores, seems to have taken everyone by surprise. Like sidewalk stalls hawking bitter melons and bok choy and lemongrass on the streets here in San Francisco, private passions, too, are spilling out with candor onto the public place. Indian writers—Rushdie, Arundhati Roy, Kiran Desai, Aravind Adiga— have become winners of one of the most prestigious literary awards in the English language, the Man Booker Prize. Japanese manga and anime—with their particular Japanese sensibilities and angst—have become the prominent genre of children's entertainment. Sushi is being sold in high school cafeterias, HMOs are now offering acupuncture, and feng shui and yoga have become household words.

All the while, unprecedented mass movements from south to north have irrevocably changed the north: salsa vies with ketchup as the top sauce; tango, Latin jazz, Jamaican reggae, and Mexican hip-hop liven up American dance floors; Spanish becomes increasingly the second language of choice; and so on.

If those in America still think of globalization as a one-way trip, that it is simply the Americanization of the rest, they should seriously think again. Even if the spelling checker of my Microsoft Word program refuses them as real words, the Easternization and Latinization of America are changing America as I type.

Obama's rise to the highest office of the land has opened the door wider to that growing public space in which Americans with mixed backgrounds and complicated biographies—Latino Muslims, black Buddhists, gay Korean Jews, mixed-race children—can celebrate and embrace their multiple narratives with audacity. He gives us license to embrace our various inheritances and to re-imagine ourselves in an America in which we are equal and at the center.

This too is America: the Hmong girl in Oakland is texting to her Mexican boyfriend in San Jose, who is on Skype with his *abuela* in Oaxaca. The teenager who calls herself Japorican—part Japanese and part Puerto Rican—and the boy who is Chirish—part Chinese, part Irish—are pushing the stroller carrying their global-village baby toward some intricate future.

No, I am not so naive as to believe we have moved into a Utopia. Fear of the Other will continue, of course, and bigotry and racism, and fighting over resources and for power. Many who believed in democracy and fair play when they were at the center find those ideas troubling when Friday's relationship with Crusoe suddenly and radically changes. Yet I cannot help but be optimistic, for is this not the original promise of America: "E pluribus unum"—out of many, one?

And if the Vietnamese teenage refugee was once overwhelmed by his losses, his inferiority complex, and by his alienation on the Western shore, the Vietnamese American writer, through his struggle to find words to redefine himself, has become a bona fide cosmopolitan. The world I live in now, indeed, requires communicating across time zones and hemispheres, traveling from one continent to another, and negotiating among different languages, dissimilar cultures, and once far-flung civilizations.

It was Defoe's conceit in his novel—published in 1719 and considered by many to be the first novel written in English—that the "savage" could only be redeemed by assimilation into Crusoe's culture and religion. It was beyond Defoe's power of imagination to see how much Friday, in time, could radically change Crusoe, and that the world of Crusoe was forever altered by having absorbed Friday.

On that fateful Tuesday, November 4, 2008, Friday spoke up loud and clear and declared himself an equal, and his voice is heard around the world. He has become the conductor of a new movement. He tells us all to dare dream big, and to re-imagine ourselves and therefore re-imagine America itself.

The old curse ends. Some internalized threshold for previously subjugated people is breached. To live in America fully these days is to learn to see the world with its many dimensions simultaneously. And where others hear a cacophony, the resident of the cosmopolitan frontier discerns a new symphony. His talent is the ability to overcome the paralysis induced by multiple conflicting narratives and selves by finding and inventing new connections between them. He refutes simplification and holds opposed ideas in his head without going crazy. He knows now it's within his powers to articulate and reshape his new world and, regardless of the color of his skin, play a central character in the script of his own making.

Swimming From The Mekong Delta

by Andrew Lam

How are you doing tonight? Hot? Yeah, sure is hot. We're having a tropical heat wave folks. So hot, it reminds me of coconut trees and thatched roof huts. It makes me think of myself as this impossibly handsome little boy playing with his dog, or, as so many of you are fond of putting it, playing with his food.

Yeah, as I was saying, I was playing with "Next Week's Menu" getting him to roll over in fish sauce and lemongrass, jump in the wok and play dead, when suddenly Mamma, right, she showed up with this bag and said, "kids, we got to blow this joint!"

Well, actually Mamma didn't say that, exactly. She said— now, listen, cuz this is from Vietnamese to English. Ok? Like with a bamboo flute going off in the background, so hear me out.

"O filial first son. From the sacred land in which our umbilical cords are buried we must take leave due to communist cruelty. They put your honorable father in the re-education camp. If we stay they'll send us to the New Economic Zone. We have no choice but to commit this forbidden sin. Please go bow to your ancestors, light incense and beg for forgiveness before we leave. And filial first son, don't forget your toothbrush."

I was seven years old. I was like, "What? What'd I do now?"

I'm telling you, it's just like Vietnamese mothers to make everything YOUR OWN GODDAMN FAULT! Think about it: The commies gonna fuck you up and send you to the New Economic Zone so you have to escape out to this big bad ocean, and somehow it's you who have to beg for forgiveness? And from DEAD PEOPLE?

Grandpa, great-grandma, oh ancestors of eight generations

back to the Chink dynasty, please forgive us. We can't clean your graves no more. Clean them your lazy ass selves. We got to go to America before the VC fuck us up the ass or put us in graves next to you all. So, okay. Good-bye.

We loaded up this fishing boat right, and move the Mekong-Deltoids to Beverly Hills. Entire clan that is. Vietnamese. Boat People. All climbing in this rickety fishing boat and when the next village saw us half of them came along, too. Hell, it's a twenty-one by six feet, so why not? When Americans say maximum capacity forty-five, Vietnamese automatically add a zero to it. You know how it is: Tell us it's a boat and we'll find a way to fit.

What? Who said that? What did we do with the dog? I see you. You so fat you're feeding me lines now? Well ... Thank you.

The dog? Hell, we tied a recipe with some lemongrass around his neck and sent him to our neighbor as a parting gift, you know, kinda like a Vietnamese version of meal on wheel? That's right, don't boo. You heard me. Seriously though, I really miss my "Next Week's Menu."

Anyway ... We live on top of each other, we sit on each other's lap, we shower together to save water, we sleep five to a bed—so no, there's no personal space cuz, hell, if there's space, there's a PERSON taking it, alright.

Crowded to a Vietnamese is not a family living in one room, that's just normal middle class. Hell, we didn't have Home & Garden Magazines back in Nam. Na-ah, we had Shanty, Thatch & Hut Newsletter.

Crowded on that boat is like it takes you from Saturday to Monday to get to the toilet, and Wednesday to get back. Crowded is if you bend down looking for your plastic slippers you'd lose your cherry. Crowded is when you have the hiccups and that fat lady a few people down from you gets multiple-orgasms.

When my siblings and me, all three of us came to America and we saw the two white kids next door playing that game Twister, we thought, phssaw, you call that a game? "It's Twister," said Suzie and her gayish brother, Leon.

"Nah ah, it's Life-On-The-Boat," my little brother and sister immediately corrected her. Then all three of us showed Leon and

Bobbie-Sue right then and there how to play it properly. Okay—so do you know how you can tell when Vietnamese boat children play Twister? We'd be like connecting red and green and yellow dots, WHILE helping each other do math homework, that's how.

Hell, it was so crowded that when them Thai pirates came and took some of us over their boat for our poontangs, the rest were thinking, "Well, at least now we can stretch our legs."

No, don't boo. Seriously though, them pirates man, I got me an AK-47 then, I'd have blown them out of the freaking water. Swear to God. Mean ass mofos. Funny thing was, there were twenty of us to one of them, and they were just opportunistic fishermen with knives and one spear gun, that was it, but we were a bunch of morons and burnouts. So crammed in, so weak, dehydrated, what have you, we just let them have our poontangs and jewelries without even so much as a protest, man. Well, I hope they rot in hell.

We were just unprepared. Period. We had no idea where we were going, no idea how long it'd take. And people would bring the craziest shit when they flee, let me tell you.

Like, listen to this. One woman brought land with her. Yeah, you heard me. I'm serious. Food and water make sense, right? Cup o noodles. Sure. But dirt? We ran out of water and food a week, and this crazy bitch was crying constantly. Man, I know shoulda felt bad for her. But honestly? I hated her ass.

She complained and complained and then when she ran out of food, we found out that last bag she'd been sitting on was no family heirloom. It was a kilo of dirt that belonged to her garden. What the hell was she thinking? I'm escaping out to sea to who knows where, but I got a bag of Vietnamese dirt? Why not rice? Or, maybe a bag of cheerios? Even them pirates were laughing at her. They tore open her bag and just shook their heads. Dirt!

Then another guy, old dude, right, he had a bonsai. It was like this old, fugly dwarf of a tree that's like a thousand years old. Then another brought keys to his house and cabinet with him. And get this—this old lady, she brought mango seeds. Mango seeds! She said she wanted to grow them wherever she was going to end up. We didn't know she got them seeds til it rained right, and they sprouted from her pockets.

We were robbed of everything and starving and thirsting to death, and can you imagine it: there's mango saplings coiling from right under the old lady's sagging tits? She should've gotten together with the dirt lady so they could grow mango trees so by the time we get to the Philippines maybe we coulda got something to eat.

Seriously though, reality is weirder than fiction. You're escaping out to sea, to who knows where, and the stats was that one out two wouldn't make it, due to drowning and starvation and pirates and the overwhelming generosity of the merchant and navy ships that honk their horns and let you wave and wave til your arms drop. So what do you take along? Rocks and a dwarf tree and mango seeds. Keys to an old cabinet—what the hell you gonna do with a bunch of damn useless keys? That's a riddle for the rest of your life, man. Rusting keys to a lacquer cabinet in a country you don't intend to ever, ever see again.

You hear Vietnamese are so damn practical, right, studying to be doctors and engineers and computer programmers and shit like that, but did any fool on that boat bring a life jacket? Hell no. A gun? A flare? Hello—Maybe a map and compass?

Nahh-Ah—That would be like THINKING AHEAD.

So—We ran out of food and water. My youngest bro, he was like three years old and he was dying. So guess what my Mamma did? You won't believe this shit but it's the godawful truth, I swear. She cut her finger and bled into my baby brother's mouth. It was gross. It was so awesome, man. Mamma fed him like he was little Vampire Lestat. She nearly died from that experience 'cuz she was already dehydrated herself, but she was not going to hear no? Nah-ah. She was not like ever gonna let him die.

That kid, right, he's all grown up now, six feet tall and as handsome as Bruce Lee, but guess what, folks, Scarrrred for life! Yearrrrs of therapy ain't gonna change da fact that Mamma gave life to him not once but TWICE, and she nearly died that second time, and he remembered it. Hell, as if she'd ever let him forget. She bled into him so he better go to med school, be a surgeon, and that's that. He majored in psychiatry and brain surgery, and I think he was like his own first patient. I gave a couch to honorable son number two so he can lie on it and take notes and talk to himself.

I mean. I'm not sure what Freud would say about it but we can safely assume that big U-Haul permanently parked outside his new house is for all of my bro's emotional baggage. She owns him man. Mamma got him wrapped around her finger now, no pun intended.

He wanted to be in a rock 'n roll band at seventeen, right, cuz he's really good with them drums, but she wanted him to be a doctor and he started to kick it back to her about American individualism and American dream and shit like that, and Mamma she just held up her finger with that little scar, and that shut him the hell up.

But she stopped saying shit like "*O unfilial son number two. The blood that throbs through your ungrateful veins is my blood, my sacrifice,*" like she used to.

Now she speaks her own version of Vietninglish. So listen.

"I bleet for chew. I keep chew alai. What four? So chew can be heevy-meetal rock-carr? No back Si Reet boi for chew. Chew be Mma Dee in-steed. No drum, no rockeen-roe. Chew lull cho Mamma, chew study ELM-MA-CAT."

My bro, he wanted to date Suzie, right, and Mamma'd be wagging like this with her finger in the air. "Ok, chew date. Mamma just go keel her sell to assk ang-cesster for four-giffness. Firost one no good. Mamma no have no-ting if chew no good numba two. But befour Mamma go, Mamma wan only one ting: give back two gallon of Mamma's blood. Okay?"

My bro, man, he'd be breaking down, weeping like a baby. "I'm sorry Mamma. I'll be a doctor. Mamma. I'll be a brain surgeon. Don't cry Mamma. I'll forget Suzie." She gets her way, my Mamma. Cuz you know why? Unlike driving in LA, I'm telling you, in my family, giving somebody The Finger takes on a whole different meaning.

Me, on the other hand, no good dishonorable first son, I am the only one who got to slap my Mamma and get away with it. Once, right, she took her favorite cocktail, Rum and Robitussin and she fainted right there on the kitchen floor. Everybody was acting like they were chickens without heads. My sister Le-Ann was doing her Prissy, ditsy maid Gone With the Wind routine: "Mamma gonna die! Mamma gonna die!" So I slapped her first to shut her up.

Did the pre-med boy do anything? Na-ahh. He froze. It was up to me—the yellow sheep, the strayed lamb, the screwed-up among scholarship kids—to become a Mamma Slapper. So I dropped and rolled. And straddled my Mamma right there on the kitchen floor and slapped her.

Wake up, Mamma, Wake up. Slap! Slap!

My siblings, they all stared: they were shocked. I looked over my shoulders and there was also this awe in their eyes. They were like, "You slapped The Saint!"

The truth was, I was doing something that they all fantasized in their deep dark, wet dreams but never admitted it: I was bitch slapping The Queen Bitch-Slapper. Mamma not only believes in corporal punishment, she holds seminars on it in Little Saigon, sort of like Confucianism and the Joy of S&M 101. "Mama sho chew love wit kain. No-oh ... Not shuega kain. Bamp-bu kain."

Mamma used the rod on our tender asses. Mamma slapped us every other week for sassing and what not. Especially Le-Ann, who needed to be slapped like every five minutes to stop peering over the fence to make goo-goo eyes at Leon. Well, I was slapping Mamma and Le-Ann she was just down right envious. I could see her wanting to get in on it. Her hand was rising in the air mimicking my slapping like she was trying to give me pointers on how to do it.

See, we barely survived and then we were shipwrecked and were like stranded on a deserted island for like a month before we got rescued. I'm telling you, that was rough. Our diet consisted of coconut, oysters, and seaweed. What's for breakfast, Mamma? Coconut.

"What's for lunch Mamma?"

"Boiled seaweed."

"What's for dinner, uncle?"

"Seaweed and oysters and coconut, now shut up!"

Oysters. Oysters and seaweed. We were lucky if we caught a fish and small crab, that was like Thanksgiving dinner.

Oysters. I swear, when you're a kid, a warm, quivering oyster was the nastiest thing you can ever imagine putting in your mouth, right. If you look real close, you can even see its membranes quivering. Why? Cuz, it's scared. It knows what's next. Nastiest shit ever.

My sister, Le-Ann, she nearly starved on Gilligan's isle, she was downright anorexic. She cried every time she had to eat an oyster. She threw up so many times cuz it was so absolutely nasty. This is her description: "It's like eating a big thick wad of somebody else's 3-day-old phlegm soaked in piss." My mother had to slap that girl to make her eat. "No, Mamma. I can't." Slap. Slap. Slap. "Ok, ok, ok, Mamma, I'll eat."

Took me years in America to get used to eating oyster again, folks. And only when it's on ice and comes with vodka and a horny, smiling chic who thinks that shit is aphrodisiac. But it's crazy. For one thing it was like why the hell do I have to pay so much money for them when we had to be slapped silly before to eat it? For years whenever I see an oyster, I get nauseated. I'd feel like I'm on fucking Gilligan's island again. Fuck that. Give me a quarter-pounder, man, you know what I'm saying?

Le-Ann, though, when she turned sixteen, it was suddenly like, "Oh my god, you like oysters? Me too! I just love oysters and champagne. Leonard. Let's go get us some oysters, oh, and yes, yes, caviar too!"

Honorable daughter number two wanted to get Leon's oysters, all right. For cute blond-haired Leon, she'd eat anything. Funny how Miss Finicky grew past puberty and, suddenly, how many nasty things she'd be willing to put in her mouth, no slapping necessary. "Oh Leon! I want your three-day-old phlegm. Yeah, give it to me!" I know what you're thinking, you people are nasty!

So back to Mamma on the kitchen floor: when I was slapping my Mamma, I was slappin' for all the horrors we experienced.

"Wake up Mamma!" Slap. Slap.

I was slapping her on the behalf of all oppressed Asian kids who had to do our homework and eat the shittiest food like catfish in stinky-high-to-heaven shrimp paste when every one else in the neighborhood had macaroni and cheese with Spam. I was slapping her on behalf of emasculated Asian boiz who grew up under the fiery breath of dragon ladies and all the teases we got for being poor FOBs. I was slapping her for making me leave "Next Week's Menu" behind.

"Wake up, Mamma!"

Oh, she woke up alright. We knew she was okay cuz she opened her eyes, right, looked at me, and with her Terminator's GRIP, she grabbed my hand in mid-slap, and she started slapping me with it.

Mamma survived. Hell, we ALL survived. The truth is Honorable Number Two did really well. And so did Le-Ann. They're doctors now.

Last year, honorable Number Two bought a big yacht. He took us all on around New Port and Corona Del Mar. We drank champagne and waved to all these skinny blond people on their yachts who looked over at us kinda funny. Why? Maybe cuz Mamma, she brought her rice cooker, and she wore her conical hat, black pajamas and Prada purse and squatted right there on the deck to make us lunch.

But so what? We ain't Fresh Off the Boat, ain't F.O.B.s no more.

We've got Fob-ulous Oriental Booties!

We're Flamboyant Oriental Balladeers!

We've got Fantastic Oto-Biographies!

It's like, look at us now, man. I mean, really look!

We're yacht people now!

ANDREW LAM is a writer and a co-founder and editor of New America Media, an association of over 2000 ethnic media organizations in America. He also contributed over 60 commentaries to NPR's *All Things Considered*. Lam was a John S. Knight Fellow at Stanford University during the academic year 2001-02, studying journalism. He has lectured widely at many universities and institutions, including Harvard, Yale, Brown, UCLA, USF, UC Berkeley, University of Hawaii, William and Mary, Hong Kong, and Loyola University. His awards include the Society of Professional Journalist Outstanding Young Journalist Award and Best Commentator in The Media Alliance Meritorious awards, The World Affairs Council's Excellence in International Journalism Award, the Rockefeller Fellowship in UCLA, and the Asian American Journalist Association National Award. He was honored and profiled on KQED television in May 1996 during Asian American heritage month. He was featured in a 2004 PBS documentary, *My Journey Home*, in which a television crew followed him back to his homeland, Vietnam.

Lam's first book of essays, *Perfume Dreams: Reflections on the Vietnamese Diaspora*, won the PEN American Beyond the Margins Award in 2006 and was short-listed for the Asian American Literature Award. His second book of essays, *East Eats West: Writing in Two Hemispheres*, was published in October 2010 and listed as a Top Ten Indie Books in 2010 by *Shelf Unbound Magazine*. His next book, a collection of short stories entitled *Birds of Paradise*, is due out in Fall 2012.

http://www.redroom.com/author/andrew-q-lam
https://www.facebook.com/pages/Andrew-Lam/83033371568

Tremors in 4 parts

by Sonia Sarkar

I. San Francisco in Spring

we are 30 miles out from the epicenter, but the first thought
that comes to my mother's mind is the way they used to duck
for cover during air drills along the Assamese border in 1971.
Safely ensconced in her arms, I feel no difference between these
tremors and the steady humming of our minivan, my favorite
cradle. As the plaster crumbles around our newly painted
doorframe, she says she has never watched me fall asleep so
peacefully, so rapidly.

II. Seattle at Solstice

I hate the waxy skin of Washington apples with a passion
But Sandy (and Jane, John and Mary) from the playground say:
that's going to have to change

My little brother bobs around our house
like he's always lived with secret passages,
window seats and rhododendrons

Me, I miss patchy green grass
Smog-tinted fish fry smell
Withering bay leaves
Seeing shiny blue stars next to my name

Living amongst all of these Christmas trees is too much like
winter every day.

III. Austin on Labor Day

I had been terrified
But as we skimmed the shiny school brochures it was like

looking at the America of 2050 everyone gestures vaguely
towards:

Target-ad rainbow kids lining up in the cafeteria
Waiting for their locally grown algae
Spooned out by smiling spirit grandmothers

Me, I keep waiting for the real Texas to pop out and whisk me
away
The one I breathe in on long drives to Dallas
As our

lone   star

soaks skins in alarming orange.
Past the Caterpillar dome, the faded Kolaches store,
The pulsing rigs and the barbed wire.

Once,
We pulled up next to a hulking Chevy.
And in slow motion: Driver glanced at us twice,
10-galloned head swiveling tipsily through the pesticide air
He rapped his hard knuckles to our window, as
I watched Ma grip the armrest tight

Twenty minutes later—
We drove away with a basket of the juiciest chandler strawber-
ries I've ever tasted,
And a sheet of Pokémon stickers transferred from his little boy
to ours.

IV. Kolkata at 9 AM

My brother and I are trying to sleep off our jetlag
But dad is all tourism fervor and childhood memories!
We arrive at the most imposing, ivory building I've ever seen—
Fittingly so
Welcome to the Queen Victoria Memorial.

A thousand young Indians are throwing frisbees on the lawn,
Blissful in the shadow of faded colonialism
Sipping Coke out of glass bottles with green straws

Looking for all the world like extras
In a sepia Audrey Hepburn movie.

In our GAP shirts,
We are cocky as American cotton,
Here only for the thrill
And the gates to the Taj Mahal require us to stand in the
foreigners' line,
Pay ten times the normal fee

My parents look remorseful,
Our glossy blue passports weighing heavily
As we envelop our shoes in sheer shower caps,
Designed to protect a world wonder from wanderers.
Sweltering under a monsoon sky we can no longer claim as
ours,

We pile in front of a royal tomb:
Peacefully.
Rapidly.

 SONIA SARKAR serves as chief of staff to the CEO of Health Leads, a national non-profit that mobilizes undergraduate volunteers, in partnership with providers in urban clinics, to connect low-income patients with the basic resources they need to be healthy. She graduated from Johns Hopkins University in May 2008 with a B.A. in public health and international studies and joined Health Leads' national office from the Baltimore site, where she served as a programs manager and volunteer. A 2008 Truman Scholar and member of the *USA Today* All-Academic Team, Sonia worked as a mayoral fellow with the Baltimore City Health Department, where she provided case assistance and studied the effects of inadequate housing on health outcomes in urban neighborhoods. In 2009, she was named SAALT's South Asian Changemaker of the Year, and also received a Rotary Cultural Ambassadorial Scholarship to conduct work with local paramedic teams in San Jose, Costa Rica. Sonia is an avid poetry fan and her work has been featured or is forthcoming in *Right Hand Pointing, the Yale Journal of Humanities in Medicine, 32Poems, Pyrta, Urban Confustions, Cerebration* and the *Journal of the Canadian Medical Association*, amongst others.

hey, chinky!
What does it mean to be an Asian American in the 21st century?

by Curtis Choy

The identity conundrum has shifted and transformed into something yellow baby boomers hadn't foreseen. Despite the 'post-racial' 'post-identity' rationalizations by defenders of white male privilege, the three main Asian groups have become many more. It feels weird to go through this again, as I had settled this for myself 35 years ago, so allow me the perversity of reviewing my own film from 1975, *DUPONT GUY: The Schiz of Grant Avenue*, to get at it.

I am a 3rd generation chinaman from San Francisco. My grandfather, a merchant, arrived in 1913 from *Jung San*. My eldest uncle was born on the ship coming over. My father was born in grandma's sewing factory on Clay Street. I was proud that she had a union shop. I'm told I spoke fluent Cantonese until age five and the start of American school. English is my language. I wouldn't find out until college that there was this other Chinese language, Mandarin, and that some Chinese people ate spicy food. And that my peeps came from a bumpkin corner in Kwantung.

My film essay argues that we are neither China Chinese nor white Americans, that we are not hyphenated and schizoid Chinese-Americans, and if we chose to define ourselves as not self-loathing and not tied to ancient foreign culture, we would choose to be called *chonks*. (That it rather closely resembles the word *chinks* may explain why it never gained widespread adoption, but those who know still hail their brothers, "Hey, chonk!")

It was 1970. Frank Chin showed up and blew everyone's mind in Jeff Chan's Language and Culture class in Asian American Studies at San Francisco State College. He put on a blackboard two columns: the Sexy, and the Not Sexy. The class filled in the lists. Everything Sexy (cool and desirable) was white. Everything unSexy turned out to be Asian. This led to an examination of Charlie Chan and Fu Manchu and WW2 anti-Jap movies, and chinx-in-space (*Flash Gordon*'s Ming the Merciless) and all of the commercial images that defined to white America what we were and were supposed to be. Up to that point, Chin figured 2500 movies had presented the vision of us as effeminate clowns and sexpot whores.

I decided that my role as a filmmaker would be to counter every one of those movies.

Frank Chin was a writer at KING-TV in Seattle. He was tall, had a long ponytail, wore his trademark denim shirt, black jeans, and Tony Lama cowboy boots. For a bunch of fledgling Chinese-Americans, Frank's presence was a revelation. He challenged us to examine Chineseness. How Chinese were we ChineseHYPHENAmericans? Why were white people so exalted? Why wasn't anyone complaining about Asian stereotypes? What were the stereotypes? Were these good or bad? Why is 5 generations of Chinaman history in America unknown? A lot of deep self-examination went on both collectively and personally. Boys and girls cried in class. Upsetting the status quo and forging a new culture that was neither China Chinese nor white American became the mission for those of us who saw ourselves as the vanguard of indigenous Chonk culture. These are the underlying foundations at the core of *Dupont Guy*. These assumptions had become so basic to me that the fact that these were the teachings of Frank Chin didn't register. 25 years later, I was inventing plausible bullshit to get a grant to make *What's Wrong With Frank Chin?* and submitting *Dupont Guy* as my sample film.

That's when I finally realized Chin's fingerprints and boot marks were all over the film.

DUPONT GUY had begun in 1972 as a film production class project at San Francisco State. It would not be finished until after I left school in 1975.

It opens with a verbatim reenactment of a racist TV news segment about "gangs in Chinatown". This was from the San Francisco ABC affiliate which basked in self-satisfaction for its invention of the "happy talk" news style. The anchorman, who gave every appearance of having made up the story off-the-cuff, was the most highly paid and arrogant in the Bay Area, and my co-conspirators feared a lawsuit if we used the actual broadcast. Lacking the technical facilities to properly do TV graphics, I improvised by drawing a picture on butcher paper and thumb-tacking it to the wall behind the anchorman. Generic B-roll of street scenes flickered until he ended his rant cum news story, " ... if the killing keeps up, sooner or later, it'll be a matter of time before a tourist couple from Kansas City that gets it, and all Hell breaks loose. It can happen. And they're hoping it won't. And so is the mayor. He wants more police down there. And it looks like the police will be beefed up in Chinatown." *The sensationalistic tone echoes the yellow journalism of newspapers, the ones that brought us the Chinese Exclusion Acts and Alien Land Laws. That only Caucasoid lives had value, and that police oppression would be relied on, was not lost on us.*

Smash cut to a blond white woman yelling out of a car window: "WHAT DO YOU GOOKS THINK THIS IS, CHINATOWN? Why don't you go back where you came from!" For those who are loathe to accuse anyone of racism, this was based on a real incident. The scene ended with tire screeches as a carload of Chinaboys gave chase, bringing us to the main titles. *The chase scene was excised but can be seen as the prologue to a*

collection of short films called Snipers in The Trees.

In 1972, I could stretch a $20 bill over two weeks; my share of the rent with 2 mates was $50 a month. A 100-foot roll of 16mm film that ran for 2 and 3/4 minutes would cost $30 for raw stock, developing, and a work print. This was a lot of dough for a working class kid. Needless to say, motion picture film was unaffordable, so I did the next best thing: I stole it. A film student friend of mine introduced me to a guy who worked as a film processor at a TV station. Back then, all TV news reportage was shot in the field with film, processed at the station's film lab, then the original film was cut, mounted on a telecine and shown during a newscast. I would go to the station on weekends, and my new pal would slip me two 400-foot rolls of film, each of which would run 11 minutes. This was fine for when I could beg and borrow a big camera, either a news film camera with built-in magstripe sound, or a silent Arriflex or Eclair sync camera that had 400-foot magazines. But what I actually owned was a fourth-hand wind-up spring-motor Bolex that could only handle 100-foot loads and had no sound. I used the TV station darkroom to spool down a big film roll into 4 little ones. It became a routine, me going in every few weeks to drop film off for free processing and swiping some free film on the way out. We called this "liberation."

A blue-tinted dawn breaks over Chinatown. Sparrows tweet.

Distant Cantonese voices are heard. Poet Janice Mirikitani recites *The Schizoid Lie*:

What is Chinese-American?
What does it mean to be Chinese American?
We've been defining what it is NOT.
It is not a blending of east and west.
That's a lot of hooey to make you jump into the melting pot theory.
We are not Chinese, and we are not American.
We are the unique, complete Chonk cultural reality in the middle of a schizoid lie.
When a chinaman says 'American,' he means 'white.'
When an American says 'chinaman,' he means 'nigger.'
When anyone says 'Chinese,' I say, "Dat ain't me."

The *Kung Fu* TV show theme plays over lens flares, and the clack of fighting sticks coincide with the movements of white people doing tai-chi in Portsmouth Square, the only public outdoor space in Chinatown. *Popular across America, "Kung Fu" was ridiculed and despised by chonks for its yellowface lead actor and fortune cookie aphorisms. It was galling to see white people doing OUR tai-chi in OUR park.*

An 'oriental' fanfare and gong has us descending into the Ping Yuen housing project. We pan across hundreds of mailboxes. A Chinatown tour guide delivers his spiel to tourists. Simultaneously, a woman earnestly interviews a suspicious project tenant known as The Chinatown Kid. "You live here, too? Do you like it?" "What do you mean, 'Like it?'" The tour guide keeps pattering. The audio layering is deliberate. She intimates the resident is a 'gang person.' He insists, "You got it wrong."

The Salvation Army wants to "Save Our Families!" They take over Grant Avenue, leading gullible Chinese-Americans in hymnals. "A Hundred Million Miracles" is appropriated from *Flower Drum Song* to mock Christianity's historic missionary hypocrisy. *It was the Christians who brought the Opium Wars to China and kidnapped girls in Chinatown in the guise of 'rescuing slave girls.'*

As giant winter melons are passed from hand to hand and descend down a chute, the tour guide drones on about United Artists, the Transamerica Pyramid, James Bond movies. Our homegrown gangster won't reveal his secret plan to make money.

Middle-aged working class chonks are seen moving boxes and carts. A '60s era language lesson hisses and scratches:

Listen, please.
I am the teacher.
You are the student.
I am an American.
You are not an American.
When I talk slowly, you understand me.
When I talk fast, you don't understand.
Now, please, answer my questions.
Am I the teacher?
Yes, you are.
Are you the student?
Yes, I am.
Am I an American?
Yes, you are.
Are you an American?
No, I'm not.
Do you understand me when I talk slowly?
Yes, I do.
And when I talk fast?
No, I don't.

"But you speak English, right?" our microphone cable-squeaking interviewer asks. *The ridiculous assumption that a non-English speaker can't be an American, or will suddenly understand English if it's spoken loudly and slowly, persists to this day.*

A butcher with a paper hat is framed by slabs of hanging meat. Grocery women select fruit. A man with a hardhat and white lab coat heaves cardboard into a dumpster, only to have them rebound. The Chinatown Kid says, "You have to wonder how come your parents haven't Made It. How come he's been a cook for about 40 years, you know," then concludes, "To Make It, you have to ... kiss up to white people. That's how you make it."

Lit red on a darkened stage, three women in shiny silk begin high kicks. The DG Striptease might sound like David Rose's "The Stripper," but it's really the "Grant Avenue" theme, slowed down to a bump 'n' grind. This satire at once mocks Asian sexual stereotypes, *Flower Drum Song*, and Chinese ribbon dancing (popular since the 'opening' of China by Nixon; the blasphemy being that the ribbon was made of toilet paper). Which leads to a Chinatown funeral parade crosscut with a Chinese New Year's parade.

Chinee culture booshit number
bumping down the street one leg shorter than the other
Seven generations of a fool's gold gum sahn dream
while chonk culture lives in exile at home

No China Chinese,
no white blonded Amer-kan

Do we hate ourselves on the sly?
Choosing, splitting ourselves apart,
Ass-milating into the melting pud dominating white culture
rejecting our women
rejecting our men
marrying white racist love?

No!
We refuse doo-doo this suicide.
"Eat a bowl of tea," said Louis Chu.
No. Eat banana split, you fool.

Who are you?

Frank Chin had predicted that the Japanese-American out-
marriage rate was so high that, within a generation, they

would show diminishing numbers. This has come to pass, and it's pretty clear that every ethnic group past its third generation in America will follow suit. We used to call these yellow/white couples "banana splits." The media depiction of the Asian man as outsider/other/loser/gangster/laughing stock has fueled their rejection by Asian women. Similarly, the desirability of Asian women by white men is imaged everywhere constantly. I was shocked by the vehement hatred of white women towards Asian women while working on a documentary about race in San Francisco.

A woman calls out in Cantonese: "Hey, who dropped this 10 dollar bill?"

The Melted Pot. The only conventional documentary shot in the whole movie is a long pan of a black and white photo, a family of seven kids, ending on poet George Leong:

> *You can't say nothing about melting pots, 'cuz the pot's all white.*
> *If you're not white, you can't melt in, in America.*

He raps about how language is used against us—our accents, our idioms held up by white society as evidence of our inferiority. Black language gets co-opted by the mainstream, but Asians are expected

> *... to stick with our ancestor's culture ... there's no way for Asian Americans, for Chinese Americans, or Third World people, to write in white language. There's always some cultural thing that feeds back to you.*

The People's Liberation Army band plays "The Sportsman's March." A dark weathered plywood fence has names chalked in white. Betty Lee Sung, Rose Hum Lee, Standford Lyman, Calvin Lee, Pearl Buck, Francis Hsu, Bessie Loo, Lin Yutang, Victor Wong, some deliberately misspelled. These are the early authors and explainers of all things Chinese in books, magazines, and movie stereotypes. These people have defined us to white America, in a way acceptable to whites. A man in a white helmet and a woman in a railroad cap cross off each name with a yellow scrawl. Charles Chan a.k.a. Charlie, S.I. Hayakawa, Run Me Shaw, Ddavidd Carradine, Gunter Barf, Jade Wong Snow, C.Y. Lee, Leong Gor Yuen, Irene Tsu. All spouting sociological psychobabble to rationalize yellow complicity in white worship. On the list are white people who presume to know us yellows by viewing us like bugs under a magnifying glass.

In a bluish kinescope of *Flower Drum Song*, James Shigeta says, "Sometimes the American half shocks the Oriental half, and sometimes the Oriental half keeps me from showing a girl what's on my mind." George Leong rejoins,

> *That's a bunch of boo-shit. You won't see me changing my voice.*

The fence names continue: Benson Fong, Keye Luke, Victor Sen Young, Nancy Kwan, France Nguyen, Tom Wolf.

> George: *I ain't got no language problems.*
> George Woo: *I ain't got no language problems.*
> Philip Ahn, Richard Loo, and Pardee Lowe get crossed off.

Are You Chinese or Chinaman? The third act begins with a hot spray of saliva in the eye and a chalkboard screech to the ear:

> *Sheeeeeit.*
> *We ain't no Chinese-Americans, man.*
> *Matter of fact, we ain't even Chinese.*
> *Let's face up to it.*
> *All of you, all of us,*
> *what we is is*

we's all chinamen,
cuz chinamen suffer and chinamen are miserable
and chinamen cry and chinamen die
Chinamen work like fucking dogs slaving night and day
Chinamen cook in kitchens, wash dishes
and kiss-ass to honkie tourists
Chinamen smile politely and no speak english-y
Chinamen 'ah-so' and tom and chinamen lie
pretending everything is fine
when everything is fucked ...

This poem by GT Wong got the program "Chinese Youth Voice" kicked off a liberal Pacifica radio station. Their excuse was the 'use of obscenity,' but they didn't like the message and didn't want to hear any more Mandarin that they couldn't understand. Documentary producer Spencer Nakasako cites GT's rap as 30 years ahead of hip hop. The handheld aesthetic, quick cuts, and close-ups of our peeps also distinguish this for its time.

Check yourself out, man
Are you Chinese or chinaman?
Yeah, you know the answer
Don't lie to yourself

All the eggheadedness of this movie culminates in GT's last lines:

We've got to get freedom
and we've got to get it now.

Beneath the final credits is a long dolly down Jackson Street as "Almond-eyed Burro" is sung, performed by George Leong and myself. The song laments the stereotype of small-dicked Asian men, and the shot ends on an inert chinaman body next to a fire hydrant. *Not exactly upbeat or uplifting, but, true to its Frank Chin lineage, no viewers were left on middle ground. They could love it or hate it, but they were compelled to discuss it.*
    That this film essay was ever completed is a testament to

chinamen chicanery, perseverance, and the spirit of truth and defiance. And a belief that PBS is not a worthy destination. At a time when no one had any home video junk, this work emerged from primordial Asian Amerikan ooze completely unfunded.

"Dupont Guy" received the Documentary Award from the Academy of Motion Picture Arts and Sciences in 1975. It received high marks for originality and content by several distributors, but was rejected as 'unmarketable.'

Yeah, I know. I didn't answer the question. Consider this to be background for those of you who want to keep redefining a moving target. I never did buy into "Asian Pacific." Why is it half the movies at Asian American film festivals come from Asia? Let the immigrants and hapas sort it out. Or else the Feds will. I will be tempted to tick "Other."

Curtis Choy's production company name, Chonk Moonhunter, is a contraction of 'chonk' and 'The Iron Moonhunter,' a legend about the mythical train built out of stolen parts from the Transcontinental Railroad by long-suffering Chinamen to take them home to China.

Dupont Guy: The Schiz of Grant Avenue is available at www.chonkmoonhunter.com

Lawson on Frank

by Curtis Choy

The following is a transcript of an interview with Lawson Inada, Poet Laureate of Oregon, conducted for the video documentary What's Wrong With Frank Chin? *in August of 2002.*

INT. BARN (LAWSON'S ATELIER)
A balsa wood model airplane wing skinned with tissue paper, mounted on a wall behind a seated Lawson Inada, lifts with the wind, and flutters down off of its nail.

CURTIS
I'm telling you, Frank is here!
So what's the story about this table?

LAWSON
Oh, he was doing some construction for me. He can make a chest of drawers. He can put in windows—if he were here now, I'd ask him to put a couple of windows in this barn and a heating system, because he knows how to do all this stuff. And so, he used this table to saw, and the way he sawed it, ah, sawed down to the top. So he made those marks. These are Frank Chin marks. (Laughs) We were taking a day off from his construction process. So went to a hobby store, and he had an airplane he wanted to build. We went in and the guy dug up this old balsa wood kit. And he says, "Boy, everything is plastic now. You sure you want to do the balsa? You going to start from scratch?" Frank says, "Yes." We got the balsa wood kit and some paper. And he creates this wing, which I keep—he hasn't finished the rest of it yet, but you know it's still a heck of a wing. When you look at the construction on this, you're like, "Man, is this put together or what?" So I keep

it around. I shift it around now and then. It just catches the air.

So one of the things that always struck me about Frank is that he has all these skills. By the time I met him he was already a professional carpenter, construction worker, and he had already been a professional brakeman on the railroad. And he had also worked as a professional filmmaker, and journalist, and film director. So he's always had all of these skills. Those of us who are his friends have always admired him for that because he could do things. Sometimes I think, boy it's too bad he wasn't in the concentration camps with us because we were just stuck in these places, like in this barn. And you had to make do. You know, if Frank was with us, he could have made the furniture. (Laughs) He could have started up a local newspaper or we would've done some publications. And he's got some kind of gifted research mind. So he'd 've probably researched the laws and maybe, you know, managed to get us out of the camps! And, not coincidentally, he's also a great cook. So, he could have worked in the mess hall and done some stuff with that junk that we were given in cans. Every so often I would joke around with him about, "Man, too bad you weren't in camp with us!"

Frank is this legendary figure. I had been living in San Francisco. I had taken a leave from University of Iowa at the writer's workshop, for a semester. And when I went back to Iowa this new guy had come into Iowa. His name was Frank Chin. You know, I never met him there. But it's a small town. People were talking about him, people that I respected as writers. And they would say, "Hey, have you met this guy Frank Chin?" I said, "No, no." So, you know, the guy is a heckuva guitarist. And he'd be playing at so and so clubs, but he's also acted in a couple of plays. And, he's a heckuva writer. He's writing fiction, you know. So I met Frank before I met him through these other people talking about him. And I've never met him in Iowa. This is about 1961, but he said this funny thing about me, because I was late getting back to Iowa. And I had gotten detoured along the way, so I came in a couple of days later than expected. Then one of my friends says, "Where have you been?" I said, "Well you know, I had to do this and that and ended up being in Louisiana." And he says, "Well there's a guy in town named Frank Chin, and he called you the Missing Chink!" (Laughs) I was the lone Asian in town. And there was a Chinese restaurant that Frank worked at, washing dishes and just hanging around because that was like the Asian outpost. And so, Frank had a presence in my life even before I met him.

By the time I met him it was about 10 years after that, around '71, where I just got this phone call one day. "Hey, this is Frank Chin. We're having a literary party celebrating the publication of this book edited by Ishmael Reed called *19 Necromancers From Now*. It's going to be in Berkeley. It's going to be at the publisher's house. It's going to be great. Why don't you show up." I said, "Uh, sure." So, my wife and I drove down to Berkeley and went to this nice house. It was a great party. I met Ishmael Reed. Alex Haley was there. Richard Brautigan. Herb Gold. Ishmael had put together this great anthology of writers. It had Victor Hernandez Cruz. It was really something. Big publisher. I think it was Random House. And then Frank came up to me and introduced himself, and he said, "Well, when this is over let's go get a pizza." I said, "Okay, let's go get a pizza." So we ended up in this place in Berkeley. There was me, and Jeff Chan, and Shawn Wong, and Frank, and maybe one or two other people. And we sat down and it was kind of like in that movie *Seven Samurai*. Where you've got the one guy who's the leader. And as soon as we sat down he says, "Okay, tell you what ... " He had a plan. And the plan ended up with Frank and Jeff and Shawn and me. We ended up being the four *Aiiieeeee!* boys. So we didn't have the Seven Samurai, but we had the four *Aiiieeeee!* boys, and that was the start of it. He says, "Tell you what, why don't we do this and that, this and that." You know, immediately I could tell that he had this leadership charisma, and he was also able to see that we all had these certain skills. Certain things that we could do, you know. Shawn ending up by making the contacts, business and things. Jeff had a good organizational mind. Frank had an overview and the plan. I was just maybe more like the Toshiro Mifune figure. From Fresno! (laughs) And so that's how that whole *Aiiieeeee!* boys thing got started. You know, within a couple of years after we had done all this research (and Frank had been researching anyways), it seemed like he had been conducting interviews on his own because he had this vision of things. We made phone calls. Boy, you think of all the writers that we found. We essentially found our past, our history. Our literary history, cultural history. Because it hadn't been known until then. We found all of these people, pretty much, living in obscurity. Maybe still trying writing careers or maybe having to abandon them. All of our elders. It's like we found all of our uncles, and parents, and aunts, and grandparents, and things like that through all these writers that are now part of the Asian American studies curriculum. But it was *Aiiieeeee!* that brought us together and enabled us to come out with that work.

But, speaking of Frank's skill ... he started the Asian American Theater Workshop. He could write the play. He could create the set. He could direct the play. He could act in the play. He could produce the posters. Tremendous amount of talent and with his mind the way it is, he had a computer mind before there were computers. Just all organized in there. You pressed the right button and all the facts and figures ... I really respected and admired that quality of his because, as a poet, I'm kind of all over the map. It's just all swirling around here. But Frank had an organized mind. Another thing that really struck me about Frank, and actually the four of us who did *Aiiieeeee!*, was that we didn't even think about money. Now that I look back, we put our money where our mouth was. Because after we made a search, a survey through our past, we found this novel. Jeff Chan found it in a used-book store. It was an out-of-print novel by John Okada, who had just passed away shortly before that. But we found his book. And we read it. And we realized that this book, *No-No Boy*, is a great novel. And here it is, languishing on shelves. It had only sold several hundred copies since it came out in 1957. And so here we were in the '70s. We got to do something about this. And, you know, in our dealings with publishers, we've never made any money because all of the other people that we published got the money, you know. All of the writers that we published in *Aiiieeeee!* or *The Big Aiiieeeee!* always got paid. In contrast to how we were treated, where people may not pay us, or would not offer us anything. But we always paid other people. And with *No-No Boy* we said, "Okay we're gonna get this published." And all the proceeds are going to Dorothy Okada, John's widow, because we had made contact with her by that time. And so, Shawn did the legwork and found someone who could have this novel reprinted. We had to dig way down and deep into our pockets. We had to come up with 600 bucks each to get that novel reprinted. And I was making around $7,000 a year at the time. Frank was between jobs. Shawn was finishing up graduate school. Jeff was just starting teaching. He was making about five or six thousand (laughs). We all had kids and stuff. So 600 bucks at that time was a big deal, but, okay, "Let's do it." 600 bucks, "You got it." I don't know where I got it from or whatever (laughs). Maybe I had to drive some retread tires for awhile or something. We just went ahead and did it. The University of Washington Press took it over from there. But, looking back, it feels good how we used to just do things because of Frank's leadership and organizational skills. We just went ahead and did it. And we were all buddies. We were all very different. Raised in different ways. So it was just very exciting and we didn't have any hassle. We just became this instant team.

We always talked about the movies a lot. Like we were kinda in the *Seven Samurai*. And the other day it occurred to me that in *The Wizard of Oz* you have the people looking for courage, people wanting a heart, people wanting a brain. And then Dorothy herself was trying to find her way back to Kansas. And I realized that they should've come to Frank because, to me, Frank had the heart, you know. He had the courage. He has the brain. And he has the sense of home on honing in on things, you know. As he always says, he's a Chinaman. He sees himself—this is home, you know. Generations of home, and now it's called Asian America. But he always saw the territory in that way. So that's a quality that I really appreciate.

Another thing that people may not know about Frank is that because of all this organizational skill and his charisma and his leadership capabilities, he put together the first Day of

1976 photo taken by Nancy Wong from set of Farewell to Manzanar, *a film by John Korty based on Jeanne Wakatsuki Houston's book of the same name. (Lawson Inada on left, Frank Chin on right)*

Remembrance, which was actually a work of theater. He and Frank Abe got together and they made calls and had meetings in Seattle, the National Guard, the police chief, etc. (laughs), etc. the Army. It was amazing. The first Day of Remembrance. And people have taken that term and used it beyond the Nikkei community. But the first one was orchestrated and directed and conducted by Frank Chin. You'd show up, and you got a name tag. So you were treated as if you were going to camp. And there was all these old, what looked like World War II buses there. And you had to get on the bus. And there were all these different army figures, military figures. We went from Seattle to Tacoma, to the fairgrounds there where the actual assembly center camp was with the Seattle people. And what they called Camp Harmony. And we arrived there. We were herded by all these military people. It was really something. I was sitting in a bus next to the guy who had been administrator of the camps in Idaho. He was telling me, "This might've been like camp for you people. I realized that, that's why one of the first things I tried to do when I became the administrator of that camp—I tried to recruit some teachers just because so many kids were arriving in busloads that I knew we had to continue some kind of education process for the duration." We went to this big assembly exposition hall in Camp Harmony. There were displays of artwork. I don't know where Frank Chin and Frank Abe found all that stuff. A lot of people have these things in their attics, including a mock-up guard tower, looked like it had been made from toothpicks and popsicle sticks. You know, when the old people were in camp they kept active. They wrote poetry. They created things. They carved things out of peach pits. There was a wonderful display, but it was pretty solemn. And there was the honor guard and the flag salute and the Pledge of Allegiance. The first speaker was Pat Morita. And he says, "Just remember, people: if it hadn't been for camp, you wouldn't be here!" (laughs). That's all he said. And everyone laughs. It was wonderful. It was a very positive day in camp because all these Seattle and Washington State dignitaries came and offered their welcome back into the community. All I'm saying is, that if it hadn't been for Frank, it wouldn't have happened.

Frank and I were both testifying about the camps in the '80s before this federal commission. And both of us recognized this name of James Omura. He was the guy who had just come and given testimony. So we waited for him to finish his talk and hooked up with him. And that opened this whole thing about the resisters. The resistance that was in camp. By talking to Jimmy, who was ... he was history. He was part of the trial having to do with the Heart Mountain resisters. But that's a good example of kinda knowing the territory and sort of keeping aware and then something happens and you have to recognize it. This is important, and we had known Jimmy's work because Jimmy was this visionary Nisei journalist and editor, and he had put together this wonderful series of issues for his magazine, called *Current Life*. And it included Asian American authors, but it included other nationally-known authors. He had a vision of us in this country, incorporated and contributing. And it was a sad story, because what happened to him was when they found Jimmy right before the evacuation, they took his press. They took away all his plates and everything. They were never recovered, and so he had the loss of that before the war. And in a way he never really regained his footing as writer because of the resisters that he had been linked with.

Another thing about Frank is that he's very generous. Okay, we never had much money, but we wanted Jimmy to come out to LA from Denver, where he was working as a landscape gardener. We flew him out, and we didn't want to put Jimmy on the couch, so I was on the couch in LA. We put him up in a hotel (laughs). You know what I mean. We took him out and wined and dined him. We were seated on the floor in the Japanese restaurant and Jimmy has a beer or two and he passes out. And Frank and I pick him up and we carry him into the bathroom where it turned out Jimmy was on some kind of heart medication. He had taken too much of it or something like that. So we called 911. I'm not saying that Frank and I saved his life, but we did carry him. (Laughs) We carried him into the bathroom of this restaurant kinda like, "Wake up, Jimmy. Hey, hey!" Put a little water on his face. "911 is coming!" And he says, "Now don't tell anyone about this." He took pride in being one of those old town journalists with the fedora.

We had all these funny adventures. Frank also knows—well, like that airplane wing shows—he knows about World War II military history, and all the airplanes, because I used to have a talk show in town and say "We have a special guest in tonight. His name is Frank Chin. He's a writer, a novelist, he's a playwright. He's going to talk a little about things." And Frank read a little bit that had to do with World War II and airplanes. We weren't a call-in show, but a guy called up and says, "Wait a minute, I beg to differ with, ah, this because the plane was FFF P8." Frank said, "No, it wasn't." Now this guy, he's a friend of mine, he's an aeronautical engineer. He knows everything. Well, Frank said, "No it wasn't because I was talking about the 1944 version which is different from the ... blah blah ... " And they went on and on. I'm sure listeners were thinking, "What IS this?" (laughs) And then this other time Frank and I were on the road, and we were driving towards LA from San Francisco. And he had this beat-up Volvo. And he wanted to go and stop at Harris Ranch, in the middle of nowhere, towards LA. They grow their own beef there, and they got this famous restaurant. But they also got this truck stop area on the side, so, of course, we went to the truck stop area inside. We were all pretty casual and crummy and everything, like truckers do. We went and sat at the counter. We ordered up a couple of things. We were sitting up and talking.

Frank was talking about all these trucks, all these trucks that he knew about. Cuz he knows all those things. So, the old trucker over here, he looked at us and says, "What kind of rig are you boys driving?" (laughs) We said, "Well, ah, it's time for us to go!" I'm sure he saw us get into this crummy old ugly little car and drive off into the sunset. (laughs) But Frank had driven that road so often. See, when he was working up in Seattle he was driving to LA and San Francisco all the time, you know. So much that, for one of his works he had created these characters off the freeway signs, see. From Harris Ranch there was this judge, his name was 'Buttonwillow McKittrick.' He was a kinda corrupt judge, but a nice fellow, you know. And then, up north, there was a sweetheart up there, 'Aurora Canby.' That's up north by Portland, in Oregon. And down in northern California, just south of Redding, was a nice woman who lived on a ranch, 'Proberta Gerber.' And then, that guy—he was in one of Frank's plays—an African American Shakespearean actor named 'Gravelly Lake Ponders.' You get towards Seattle you can go out and meet him!

A lot of people say things about Frank who haven't read his work. And all I'm saying is, you look at his work and everything that I talked about is in his work. The knowledge. The tremendous skill, the constructive skill, the creative use of language, the courage, the heart … it's all in his work. The way it is in this country, sometimes the media or publisher, they get somebody to teach so-and-so person. And Frank's work has never been taught, so as a result he doesn't have any spiffy commercial labels on him. But at the same time, I don't see how anybody could not respect his work and learn from it. But they have to read it, you know.

Now, there are hundreds and thousands of Asian American writers. But they are in another space, they're in another kind of generation, or whatever you call it, mindset. Back then, we were literally trying to find the territory we discovered. We didn't invent anything, but we just searched out what we already had. Maybe it says a lot about us as a people, or about people in general, that sometimes they get misled or they get lazy. And they really don't go through the work. I remember being with Frank at a literary conference one time. I don't think people had read his work, but they asked him why he wore those cowboy boots, you know what I mean? It's kinda like asking me, "How come you drive in THAT?"

What's Wrong With Frank Chin? is available at: www.chonkmoonhunter.com

CURTIS CHOY is an independent producer and film worker contributing to numerous independent and PBS documentaries, commercials, and feature films as a production sound mixer. He is the director of *The Fall of The I-Hotel*, *What's Wrong With Frank Chin?*, and *Manilatown is in The Heart— Time Travel with Al Robles*. His sound can be heard in *The Joy Luck Club*, *Better Luck Tomorrow*, and Academy Award winner *Breathing Lessons*.

www.chonkmoonhunter.com
www.beforeiforget.org

Flips of Fury

by Marivi Soliven Blanco

In Manila's polite society, one learns to swallow indignation over minor slights. One may leave less of a tip to a less-than-wonderful waiter, but rarely does a restaurant patron actually demand to speak to the manager. Likewise, one does not usually complain when one's rights are being trampled, whether the issue is indifferent service or obnoxious treatment at the hands of strangers. *Pasenya* (be patient) and *Hayaan mo na* (let it go) tend to dictate the rules of non-engagement between boors and their victims.

Raised in an atmosphere of genteel repression, I was singularly ill-equipped to defend myself when I first came to the United States, a country in which every other person seems ready to raise hell over the smallest inconvenience or perceived insult.

When a taxi driver loudly berated me for not having anything smaller than a $20 bill to pay with (he claimed to have no change), I simply got out and asked a nearby policeman to intervene. When a woman shoved past me in the cashier's line at the grocery, then chided, "Don't push me! I don't like being pushed!," I remained silent.

Such incidents built up an inner reserve of spite, although it took a few years before resentment led to actual self-defense. Before sharpening my own claws, I took pointers from friends and relatives who had gone ahead.

One aunt bared her fangs even before coming to the United States. When a condescending consul at the US embassy in Manila was on the verge of refusing her a visa, she snapped, "Well then don't give me the stupid visa. You think I'm dying to go to your country, but I really couldn't care less. What does your country have that we don't? You can keep your damn visa!"

At which he replied, "Why, that's exactly the kind of attitude we want from people coming to America!" She received her visa that same day.

One friend told of a more harrowing experience that occurred at the height of rush hour on a New York subway train. That evening, the car she boarded was so full of commuters that she was squeezed against a fat white woman. Each time the train stopped and started, Chit couldn't help jostling her neighbor's sizeable tummy, to the latter's mounting irritation.

When yet another commuter squeezed on board, he inadvertently pinned Chit against the lady. At this point the woman declared, "Stop pushing my stomach!" And soundly slapped her.

Chit was stunned into speechlessness. To make matters worse, the crowded car forced her to remain fused to the indignant belly. However the man who had just boarded said, "I saw what happened. You really should sue that woman."

Though she was hardly interested in a civil suit, Chit replied that yes, she was considering filing a complaint, at which the slapper began to look most uncomfortable. Sometime later, the woman got off at her stop and the rest of Chit's commute proceeded uneventfully.

One of the highest rated afternoon shows on television is a court drama called *Judge Judy*. The pettiness of some of the cases is amazing: an ex-roommate's failure to remove her belongings, prescription glasses broken while slam-dancing at a concert, the splashing of a child with paint. The fact that such disputes are entertained in a small claims court, require mediation by a witty if acerbic judge and actually merit televising, indicates that some Americans will do anything to get even with someone who has offended them.

Who needs Judge Judy when you can scold a boor yourself? During my first visit to New York, old college friends invited me to a picnic in Central Park. Luciano Pavarotti would be singing in a rare free performance and the afternoon promised warm, sunny weather.

Eager to take advantage of a free opera, New Yorkers began

staking out picnic places at first light. When we arrived by mid-afternoon, the area was carpeted with tree-to-tree blankets pinned in place with plastic lawn chairs, baskets of food, and people sprawled in various configurations of defend-our-view repose. There was barely room to walk between each spread and we were forced to step on blankets, to the annoyance of their occupants.

At one point, I timidly asked the woman sitting on it if she minded moving her blanket aside so that I wouldn't step on it. "No I won't!" she snapped, glaring at me. There was nothing else to do but step on her precious plaid. She promptly elbowed me on the shin. Ignoring the jab, I hurried after the others.

We finally found a few square feet of grass for our little group, just minutes before the concert began. Suddenly a woman stood up to get a better view of the stage, blocking those of us sitting behind her. Dozens of people yelled at her to sit the hell down. She folded her arms, ignored the complaints and remained standing.

E.'s mother, on vacation from her Manila law firm, finally hollered, "I think you need psychological help." We could not figure out why Tita V.'s remark worked so well, whether it was embarrassment or the sudden realization: *Now everyone knows what my problem is.* Whatever it was, the woman sat down and stayed seated till the end of the show.

Years later, I continued to labor under the naive impression that passivity was the best route. At one Chinese New Year Parade in San Francisco, we endured the boorish behavior of a drunken white man. Between floats he swilled beer from a bottle in a paper bag and made un-funny jokes about Ms. Chinatown and her court. When a class of martial arts students paused to demonstrate swordplay, he cocked an index finger and pretended to gun down the nearest boys: "Go ahead son, grab a sword, I got you covered," he kidded his eight-year-old.

I left, seething but silent. After dinner that night, my husband and I walked with some friends through nearly empty Chinatown streets. As we passed a trio of teenagers, I heard another white man say, "Stupid fucking Chinatown prostitutes."

I stopped and turned back. "You idiot!" I hissed. His two

female flunkies sneeringly repeated, "You id-ee-yut!" I considered turning back and saying more, but held my tongue. After hearing about both incidents, my husband explained that such people had the nerve to say such things in the middle of Chinatown because they believed they would not be challenged. They would have been less cocky in an African-American or Latino neighborhood.

Back in Oakland, another friend was treated to direct insolence when he refused to give money to a panhandler. Infuriated, the woman tried to splash him with her soda, yelling, "Go back to China where you belong!"

O. came right back and hollered, "Get your ethnicity right, lady—I'm Filipino, not Chinese!"

Fighting back was a hard but necessary lesson to learn. Years of watching other Pinoys stare down rude Americans inspired me to assemble an arsenal of caustic comebacks, all-purpose profanities and a glare that stops aggressors at fifty paces.

Though far from trigger-happy, I was compelled to fight back just this afternoon. My husband and I were driving into a parking lot when a car pulled out just ahead of us, vacating a prime spot. John immediately began signaling for it, seconds before a woman further down began signaling for the same space. John slid into the spot as our parking competitor glared at us. As luck would have it, another car backed out of a space directly in front of the grocery, providing the woman with an even better spot.

Nevertheless she was enraged. As we walked past her car, she rolled down her window and snapped, "You know I was supposed to get that spot, but never mind, whatever—stupid Chinese!"

Almost without thinking, I turned on her and yelled, "He's not Chinese, you dumb bitch!" And gave her the finger.

Five minutes later as I picked over ham hocks and chicken thighs, the woman caught up with me. She could have been almost pretty ten years ago, but a foul temper and too many peroxide episodes had creased the face and ruined the hair. Rattling her cart up to mine she scolded, "The next time you give me the finger, you'd better point it at yourself!"

"Oh no, I think you deserve it," I retorted. "Go back to your trailer park, f------g white trash. You'd better leave before I hit you!" Declaring she'd call the police on me first, she hurried away. Before catching up with his mom, her 12-year-old son looked back sheepishly and said, "I'm really sorry about this." Apparently such confrontations were nothing new to him.

Onlookers were aghast, but as I walked off, a rotund white man remarked, "Well, once they bring out their 'oppressed minority' thing, what can you do?"

The fool should have looked before opening his mouth. He was speaking to an African-American butcher.

Mistaken Identity:
Pale does not equal white
by Marivi Soliven Blanco

Filipinos are color-confused. We spent 400 years as a Spanish colony and 50 more under America as the Asian version of Puerto Rico. All that time under the white man's thumb taught us that, Obama notwithstanding, pale skin equaled power, wealth and a vastly superior gene pool.

My mother bragged that she was the only dark-skinned daughter-in-law to produce a pale child, a coveted *mestiza*. In any other country, a *mestiza* would be scorned as a 'half-breed' but, Filipinos, befuddled by their residual colonial mentality, consider it a mark of prestige. After all, some of the richest families in the country are *mestizo*, with ancestral lines that stretched back to Spain. For decades, the biggest movie stars were *mestizo* as well, and they frequently chose Hispanic screen names like Gloria Romero and Rogelio de la Rosa, to suggest a more glamorous provenance.

Every now and then, an enterprising performer turns darkness to their advantage usually by pandering to, rather than challenging, the Filipino fondness for pale skin. One Amerasian comedienne highlighted her African American features by choosing the stage name Whitney Tyson and then proceeded to build a sitcom career on jokes about her ebony skin. She sometimes swapped punch lines with an albino man called Redford White.

While Whitney Tyson won local fame by parodying herself, she would not by any stretch have been considered a matinee idol and was certainly not a figure that the average Filipina would want to emulate. That is the province of an array of movie stars, socialites and celebrities who owe at least some of their fortune to the pallor of their skin.

The poster child for the pale-skin-equals-success paradigm is Julio Iglesias's first wife, Isabel Preysler, mother of European pop singer Enrique Iglesias. Isabel is an alabaster-skinned *mestiza* beauty from our southern islands who famously married Julio Iglesias in the early '70s. She later traded him in for two more marital upgrades that propelled her into Europe's social stratosphere. These days she hobnobs with Prince Charles and Victoria Beckham and no one ever mentions her Philippine origins.

Even this Brahmin caste is ruled within by a hierarchy of 'pretty' with varying degrees of *mestiza*-hood. The *mestizang hilaw* or 'raw mestiza,' sits lowest on the totem pole because despite her fair skin, her other features (a low-slung nose, coarse black hair) are more 'native' than Caucasian. Above her perches the *mestizang intsik* or 'Chinese *mestiza*' whose eyes detract from the alabaster skin. The true *mestiza* brandishes the prized genetic endowments of her Western forebears: a straight, high-bridged nose, large eyes and brown hair. She is unseated only by the *Tisay* or foreigner.

I learned about this tacit pecking order the hard way, when someone described me as *mestiza* while chatting with a male acquaintance. He glanced at me and smirked. "But she's not *mestiza*," he scoffed. "She's just *mestizang intsik*."

That was a relatively gentle putdown compared to the teasing my dark-skinned sibling endured through childhood. Until our father put an end to the jokes, my cousins routinely called my brother 'nigger.'

That's the odd thing about Pinoy humor: it borrows the worst American slang and uses it, unfettered by historical guilt.

Filipinos' abiding obsession with paleness has led to a wide range of cosmetic options, from bleaching soaps and creams to the Filipino version of the tanning salon: the "Full Body Power Bleach Spa." I've never entered such an establishment, but I assume you strip to your skivvies, then roll along on conveyor belts like a dirty car as power hoses sandblast every speck of native pigment until you emerge on the other side, raw and translucent as a peeled radish.

Newly drained of melanin, you could then visit the New You

Clinic for the patented 'Goretex Nose Lift' to get your nostrils narrowed. Complete the package with the 'Double Eyelid' operation, where they do surgical origami on your lids to produce a deep-set Caucasian eye.

Clearly not everyone opts for surgical intervention. Nevertheless, Filipinos who migrate to America feel an intense need to become one with Anglo society, often shedding their names faster than the open-mouthed vowels that mark their homegrown accents. Gaudencio becomes Dennis, Tonay turns into Toni May. Even I changed my name for convenience's sake. Most white folk can't say Marivî—but they do remember West Side Story and " ... Maria ... I've just met a girl named ... ."

Socially, the fastest way to go pale on the color scale is to marry a non-hyphenated American—someone whose family was vaguely Scandinavian five generations ago. So my uncle was enraged when his eldest daughter married a Cuban-American. "For God's sake," he thundered. "Couldn't she at least have married a white guy?"

Having enjoyed the lifelong 'paleface advantage' back in Manila, I thought that I had somehow transcended this color issue. But soon after beginning grad school in Boston, a Latina friend quickly reminded me of the Stateside reality: "Don't kid yourself, *chica*," she snapped. "It doesn't matter how pale your skin is—you will always be colored in America."

If only she could have delivered that message to everyone back in the Philippines. So deeply integrated into our cultural psyche is this fascination with fairness that even our first colonizers poke fun at it. In Madrid, children eat a cookie that features two chocolate wafers embracing a vanilla cream core—a Castilian version of Oreos.

In Spain, those cookies are called Filipinos.

MARIVI SOLIVEN BLANCO has taught writing workshops at the University of the Philippines, Diliman, the Ayala Museum, the Museo Pambata, and the University of California at San Diego. Short stories and essays from her 15 books have appeared in fiction anthologies and textbooks on creative writing. Her writing first gained recognition with two silver medals for children's fiction at the Carlos Palanca Memorial Awards for literature in 1992 and 1993. In 1998, a short story for adults won the Philippines Free Press Grand Prize for fiction. Her first novel, *In the Service of Secrets,* was awarded the Grand Prize for the Novel in English at the 2011 Palanca Awards. It is set to be published by NAL Penguin Books in May 2013. She has served on the board of San Diego Writers, Ink since 2009.

Pinoy Heroes

by Robert Francis Flor

I waited in our old Pontiac while my father disappeared into the gray tenement. Since this was our weekend ritual, I knew that he wouldn't be long. Soon, he emerged with my Uncle Eddie and Uncle Pablo.

My "uncles" were actually bachelor Pinoy men from our community who had immigrated to the States to fill the need for field, factory and other temporary low-wage workers. American businesses needed them to replace Chinese and Japanese laborers who were excluded through the Chinese Exclusion Act and the Gentlemen's Agreement. Because the Philippines was an impoverished country, many Pinoy men came for a better life, drawn by the prospect of work or education. I didn't know it at the time, but few Filipinas were allowed into the States. In addition, anti-miscegenation laws and social standards made it illegal or unacceptable for Filipinos to marry or consort with whites (my parents ignored these prohibitions). Many of these single Pinoy men attached themselves as Manongs or "uncles" to Pinoys with families.

"Hello, Manong!" I greeted each uncle.

I was twelve and we were going to watch baseball at Sick's Stadium. My uncles always treated me.

They wore immaculate cardigans and freshly pressed slacks. Their shoes shone from a fresh buffing and they smelled of pungent cologne. They'd transformed from the janitors or restaurant workers they were during the week. They were elegant!

Dad never drove directly to the ballpark. We always stopped for lunch at Al's Casino on Second Avenue, a few blocks from the union hall that processed Filipinos for the Alaskan canneries. It was a small, brick building on the edge of the Pioneer District.

The men hung out there waiting to be dispatched. Al's was popular for its Filipino favorites—adobo, rice, pancit ... almost as good as Mom's.

The Casino lay below street level, down a flight of unlighted stairs. We entered between two pawnshops with windows full of watches, guitars, and jewelry, cast off by the desperate.

We descended the shadowed stairwell to the combination restaurant and pool hall. Mahogany men filled the cigar-permeated room. Small groups sat chatting. Some shot nine-ball. Others played rummy at tables scattered throughout the room. Sparse lighting emanated from shaded lamps, hanging from the ceiling. Odors from cigars, cigarettes, cologne and cuisine blended, saturating the air. We crossed the room and sat at the narrow, wood-paneled counter. It wasn't long before a few men drifted over.

"Tst! Bicente, dis your boy?" they asked my father in accents thick and muscular as the carabao plowing rice-fields in their distant island barrios.

After nodding "yes," my father, Pablo, Eddie and the others slipped comfortably into Tagalog—relief from their broken English. I listened, not understanding.

"You e't?" they questioned me.

"Adobo! Inihaw!" They ordered the savory marinated meat dishes though I hadn't responded. "And Chinese broccoli." My nose crinkled.

"It's good por you!" my father injected, knowing my aversion to vegetables. This was his constant admonishment to my siblings and me whenever we'd turn our noses up at any food. That or he'd launch into a story about the poor orphans in the Philippines.

"More rice, cook!" they called. "We hab a growing boy here."

"You like beisboll?" another queried, placing his strong hand on my shoulder.

I nodded. "We're going to see the Rainiers, today."

"Who's your paborite player?"

"Balcena!" I smiled. I knew "Bobby Balcena" was the correct answer. The "Filipino Flyer" played outfield for the Seattle Rainiers in the mid-'50s. He was the community's hero and mine. He would appear at Washington Hall or the Hong Kong Restaurant with Fred Hutchinson to autograph souvenir baseballs for kids when the Filipino community held events. I'd been lucky enough to have a signed team photo. I hoped to play baseball just like him when I grew up.

"You go to school?" someone changed the subject.

"Yes. Sixth grade at Immaculate."

"What you study?"

"Reading, arithmetic, language ... I really enjoy reading."

"Good," said one. "I nebber hab dat chance. Always go to da pields ... pick asparagus in Calipornia ... salmon in da canneries. Alaska! Blood money! Here's somet'ing por your education." He slipped five dollars into my hand. "I jus' gam'boll, anyway."

"Thank you, Manong." I tucked the money into my pants.

"I nebber hab dat chance, boy," he whispered. He returned to playing pool across the room.

An hour slipped passed. My father and uncles completed lunch and their conversation. They shook hands with their compadres. "Mabuhay, goodbye. See you next week."

Some followed us to the stairwell but no further. It was as if they faced another sad prohibition from fully engaged lives. They shrunk slowly back to their games of pool and rummy ... occasionally peeking over their shoulders to catch a departing glimpse. Others returned to the lonely counter ... to the comfort of shared dialect. We climbed the stairs to warm light and clear air, leaving behind the crowded purgatory. My father, Uncle Eddie, Uncle Pablo, and I left for the ballgame. We went to sit in the sun.

NOTES

Pinoy: slang term for Filipino.

Manong: the Pinoy term for a respected Uncle. It's something of a term of endearment for early immigrants who came to the United States from the Philippines. These bachelor men often attached themselves to a Filipino family. During the holidays, my dad always invited several of his compadres (town mates from Iloilo, Philippines) for dinner. He didn't want them to spend Christmas or the holidays alone. Many of them became "godfathers," which is very important in the Filipino community. It built an important spiritual connection between a family, the children and the men and women chosen as the godparents.

Pancit: a popular Filipino dish of pan-fried noodles with chicken, pork, shrimp, cabbage, carrots, garlic.

Slimer: In an Alaska fish house, the fish are initially sorted by species (Kings, Chums or Dogs, Silvers or Coho, Reds or Sockeye, Pinks or Humpies). This is hard manual labor conducted by "sorters." Each day they might sort 500,000 salmon by type into large holding bins. The fish are transferred to smaller bins above the butchering machines. Three butchers operate each machine. One opens the small bin using a pneumatic lever allowing salmon to slide onto a table. That butcher quickly organizes them in rows so the next butcher can place each on the chained conveyer belt where fish heads will be removed. The fish proceed down the belt and fall into a v-shaped slide. The butcher at the end of the belt pushes the fish into a rotating drum with teeth that snatches their tails and pulls the carcasses around the drum, gutting and de-finning them. Their bodies fall onto another conveyer belt that dispenses them on a sliming table where the slimers remove any remaining entrails, blood, fins or sores using a special hand-knife. I spent four summers in King Cove, Alaska, as part of a Filipino crew. Although I learned almost every job in the cannery during that time, I primarily butchered, drove the lift, and long-shored. Butchers and sorters received the most pay. I began as a slimer, which paid the least.

Inihaw: My mom, an American of German, Irish, English descent, became one of the best Filipino cooks in the community. She learned almost everything about Filipino cooking and improved on it. She was fondly included in the Filipino Women's Club, and when she was passing, they came often to see her and bring her communion. Here is a recipe for Inihaw, generously shared by Uncle Bob Santos:

Inihaw
1 lb pork shoulder or pork butt
1 ripe tomato
3 green onions
1 garlic bud
1 tablespoon oil
½ cup soy sauce
   1) Cut pork into cubes
   2) Cut tomato ½ inch cubes
   3) Cut green onion desired lengths
   4) Chop garlic (dice)

Mix fresh tomato and green onions in bowl and set aside. Heat wok with oil and garlic.

Stir fry pork in wok over high heat. When pork starts to sizzle, splash in 2 tablespoons of soy sauce. Let pork sizzle in soy for 1 minute. Splash 2 more tablespoons of soy sauce until sizzles.

Pour rest of soy in wok until sizzles. Pour contents into bowl with fresh tomatoes and onions. Serve hot over rice.

Adobo: a popular Filipino dish made from chicken or pork prepared in a marinade of vinegar, peppercorns, bay leaves, soy sauce, and garlic.

This recipe for Adobo is generously shared by my brother, Michael Flor.

Basic Chicken Adobo

3-4 pounds chicken pieces: wings, thighs, legs (I think the breast pieces are too dry)
1/2 c. vinegar
1/2 c. soy
1-2 small bay leaves
lots of garlic
freshly ground pepper
a little water if sauce begins to dry out while cooking

Put everything in a pot. Heat slowly and do not stir. Bring to boil then reduce to simmer. Once chicken is cooked, remove from pot to warm plate and cover with foil. Heat pot to reduce sauce. When reduced, put chicken back in to coat with sauce.

Serve with large-diced tomato flavored with patis (fish sauce) and rice.

Four Poems
by Robert Francis Flor

The Arrival

At my bus stop,
a homeless man
lounges across the shelter bench
draped with coarse blanket,
protection from morning's cold and rain.

Drenched,
I stand in drizzle
rather than intrude
on his makeshift bedroom.
a put-upon courtesy.

I mutter silently and grouse.
The rain washes
my irritation.
The bus will come
I will go with others
to warmth and comfort.

Chinese Apothecary

Wellness formulas fail. I languish in hospital hallway awaiting
x-ray. Dr. Yung prescribes Vicodin but cough persists. Aunt
Florida advises Chinese remedy.

I wander the International District to dim-sum and chow-mein
aromas. Herb and medicinal stores nest among tenements. Ginger, *hong zao* bottles and ginseng glut counters. Aisles clutter
with cardboard cartons of dried mushrooms and lotus seeds.

A Chinese pharmacist motions to shelves of Asian magic.
"You need Loquat. All loquat."

I select box decorated with hànzi, sampan, steam locomotive
and two elderly herbalists.

Qi lies within.

The Plagues

We ascend the hill in darkness
through frigid morning drizzle
past the shadowed, sullen
gauntlet of locust people
mired in the mud below.
Lice-plagued men and women
asleep in their stench,
unsheltered and oblivious
to the smell of stale urine
rising from the steps.
Heads lowered,
we avoid their blemished, cattle-boiled faces,
as we leapfrog puddled pavement
to the sanctuary of our comfort cubes.
Day passes uneventfully and
when the primal light recedes,
we descend to the streets below
cross the flooded septic Styx.
We traverse these same unwashed and fallow
whose lives are spent in traded blood
drinking the death of discards.

Theirs, the endless hunger
of tormented souls,
salved only by begged breadscraps,
time and death.

We pass without notice
or compassion.

Parallel

Elderly Vietnamese woman
dips gloved hands into street recycle bin.
She fishes aluminum cans.
Stomps each flat.
Places her catch in cloth sacks
hung from a bamboo length.
Slinging pole over shoulder,
she vanishes down street.
In old country,
she fetched water for survival
with the same skill.

ROBERT FRANCIS FLOR, Ph.D. is a Seattle native raised in the city's Central Area and Rainier Valley. He is a graduate of Seattle University and the University of Oregon. His poems have appeared in the *Soundings Review*, *Four Cornered Universe*, *4 and 20 Journal*, the *Wanderlust Journal*, the *Tamafyhr Mountain Poetry Review*, *Poets Against the War*, the *Seattle Post-Intelligencer* (2005), and the *Field of Mirrors* anthology (2008). He is currently crafting his first chapbook of poems. Robert is also developing plays based on the Filipino community in Seattle. His first play, *Daniel's Mood—Mestizos*, was published in 2011. *Daniel's Mood* was selected for a Studio Lab at Freehold Theatre and *The Teachers* was read by Seattle Cold Readers in 2010. He graduated from the Artist Trust 2010 EDGE Writers Development Program.

Blog: http://pinoyseattle.blogspot.com/
Webpage: http://bobflor.com/

Face & Body, Mind & Heart
by Zach Katagiri

In preschool I learned that the world is not black and white. It's black, white, yellow, and confusing.

I came home from school one day with a question. "Mom ... am I ... Chinese?"

"No ..."

"Am I ... Korean?"

"No ..."

"Humph! I TOLD my friends, but they didn't believe me!"

"Oh yeah? What did you tell them you were?"

"I told them I was WHITE!"

Mom just laughed.

That was the day I learned that there was a type of person called "Japanese," and that I was one of them.

I have four names. Zachary. Aaron. Shigeru. Katagiri. A 50-50 split between English and Japanese. But I only have one identity—and defining what that identity is has, at times, been confusing. How do you weigh the gravity of culture, blood, history, and peer group, balancing self-perception with outward appearances?

When I was 10, I participated in a basketball camp. There was another Asian boy there, and we became friends. We weren't the biggest kids on the court, but when you don't miss a shot, who needs a rebound? It was fun. We rocked.

One day while we're warming up he asks me, "Hey—what kind of Asian are you? You Korean?" I shook my head. Proudly, from lessons learned, I piped up, "I'm Japanese."

He immediately jumped back and gave me a suspicious look. "You're not gonna pull out a gun and shoot me are you?"

I stood, dumbfounded. I was excited to know that I wasn't

white. I had no idea where guns and killing came into play.

At home that night, I asked my parents why a Korean boy might be wary of a Japanese and got another lesson.

I also learned that the Japanese had their own grievances to bear.

In 8th grade I had to interview a family member. I chose my Grandpa George, a second-generation Japanese American who had lived through World War II and the Internment. As an inexperienced reporter, I didn't have too many interesting questions to ask.

"State your name, please."

"When were you born?"

"Where were you born?"

"What were your parents' names?"

"What was it like growing up with parents who did not speak the same language you used in school?"

"What did you like to do in your spare time?"

Despite my feeble efforts, my grandpa is a natural story-teller and his life began to unfold before me in vivid colors. He regaled me with stories that contrasted his life before the war, to his experiences in the Internment camp, and then to the post-War reality of a Japanese American veteran returning to Oregon.

He remembered how, before the war, he had delivered newspapers for several years, saving up for a bicycle—a bicycle that had hardly seen its maiden voyage when he had to leave it behind since he could only bring with him to the camps what he could carry in a suitcase.

He told me about his parents' business that had to be given away because they had no means to up-keep it while they were in the camp. He explained how *Japanese Americans*, despite being US citizens, were denied legal due process even though it should have been their constitutional right.

He remembered standing inside the chain-linked barrier at the Portland Assembly Center where the Japanese were detained before being shipped to the Internment facilities. He saw one of his white friends from school driving by. They smiled as they always had. They waved as they always had. But he understood that they were now in separate worlds.

He talked about re-entering the post-War world with nothing. He talked about the racism that was still very much alive, the kinds of jobs he was forced to take, and the apartments that would suddenly no longer be available once his disembodied voice over the phone was linked to his Japanese face when he appeared in person.

At the end of the long interview, my hands shiny with pencil dust and tired from all that writing, he asked me: "After all you've heard about what America did to the Japanese, how do you feel about it? Do you forgive them?"

His question took me by surprise. It was one of those moments where I had to quickly search my soul, hoping to find a smart response to something I probably *should* have been thinking about, but hadn't. I did a quick self-analysis of some very basic points. Namely:

1) What kind of person am I? Hmmm ... a nice guy? That's what everyone says at school – and that's something that I am happy to aspire to be. And ...

2) Do nice people forgive other people? Or course!

And so without (much) hesitation I told my grandpa, with all the feigned confidence and nonchalance I could muster, "Oh yeah. Of course. I forgive America."

I remember looking into my grandfather's eyes anxiously, searching to see if I had said the right thing—but his smile was enigmatic. He nodded, expression wholly unchanged, and said only, "It's always interesting for me to hear young people's reactions. I get all kinds, you know."

He went on, "Well, I guess the one point that I would want to make very clear is that, despite our appearance, we are American. You are American, your mom and dad are American, and I am American. We were all born here, and that entitles us to the same rights as everyone else here. But in addition, we aren't *just* American, we are *Asian American*. And so in addition to the rights that we have as Americans, we also have a culture and a heritage that is unique to us: an experience that is uniquely ours, one that we should remember and carry with us as we go through life."

It was a seed. And it would take many years before that seed would really grow into any form of understanding, but it had at least been planted.

But even as I became more and more aware of the theoretical "fact" that I was Asian American, at the core of my self-perception was an identity formed through looking outward. And although my hometown had occasional instances of diversity, by and large, I saw whiteness.

I went through periods of rebellion against the stereotypes I thought might associate me too closely with *Asian* America, excelling in English more than math, playing sports rather than studying, and taking up the drums rather than the piano (at least until I found a way to rationalize that playing non-classical piano wasn't so Asian).

I ignored the Asian crowd and ate lunch with football players (all white guys at my school). And I even remember one day at lunch, pointing over to a table with all the immigrant Asian kids, speaking in their native tongues. Among them was a white kid, eating in silence, probably finding a haven of anonymity among the foreign. I stuck my nose in the air and turned to my friends, pointed and, rhetorically asked, "What's wrong with *that* picture?"

They looked. And laughed. Looked at each other. Laughed again, and then one of my closer buddies piped up.

"But Zach ... look at *this* table."

I did, eventually, begin to accept my Asian-ness. I even went through a period when I sought it out, as if it was some kind of elusive dragon-tattoo-birthmark that had peeled itself off my body and was off somewhere, zipping about until I could recapture it.

When I was a junior in college, I spent 8 months studying abroad in Japan. I put down a fork and knife and ate with chopsticks. I wrote music in Japanese and when I posted them online, I credited them as Shigeru Katagiri. I decided to label all the songs I had done in English during that period as songs by Zachary Aaron.

I learned the Japanese language and pleaded with the world to see Asian men as more than just computer geeks and martial artists.

I thought about the culture. I studied up on the history. I looked around at the reality of Japan as a living, breathing, changing society. I thought about how all of this applied to me—what it meant that these were my roots, and how my own family (and therefore my own upbringing)—had been influenced by all of the things that I was now experiencing in Japan on a daily basis. I tried to feel all of it coursing through my veins, because I knew it must.

But when my Japanese home-stay father would introduce me to his friends, he would always say, "This is Zach. He has the face and the body of a Japanese, but he has the mind and heart of an American."

And when I came home from Japan, although I can confidently say that I was a different person—I don't think that that person was necessarily any more Japanese.

Zachary. Aaron. Shigeru. Katagiri. A near-perfect 50-50 split between English and Japanese.

I am currently living in New York and feel lucky to be making a living in music, film, and web-design.

I write songs that sound like every other pop-song in America. I write them in English, because that's the tongue with which I can best express myself—the language of my mind and my heart.

For the sake of my face and body, I hope to make films that can contribute to a more progressive image of Asians in general, and Asian males in particular.

I build websites—broadcasts to the world—but for other people's visions because I'm still searching for my own.

I still struggle to find focus and direction.

I still think about the things I do and how they define me.

I wonder how much agency I can even have in defining myself.

Looking up and down the New York City streets, I see that this city has become a melting pot of culture, identity, values, and history. I am *in* this city—can I be *like* this city? Can I let the legacy of my heritage and the immersion of my present intertwine to move forward in tandem toward a future that acknowledges, respects, and embraces them both?

I grew up surrounded by white people—speaking as they did, loving the things they loved, embracing the culture that they made, but it didn't change the color of my skin or the blackness of my hair.

If you saw me in a crowd of Tokyo businessmen, thick in a morning rush hour, you would find me to be indistinguishable from everybody around me, yet I am sure that they would know the difference. They would sense my American mind and heart.

And I keep coming back to my grandfather's words: the way he stressed that he was not just American and realize that I, too, am an *Asian* American. Asian, yet *American. Asian American.*

ZACH KATAGIRI was born in Hawaii, grew up in Oregon, studied in California and Kyoto, Japan, and now lives in New York (Upper West Side). He has been working in digital media for the past 5 years, doing audio and video production, graphic design, and web design and development (http://www.zachkatagiri.com). He is currently the Director of Web Development and Marketing at New Hope Fertility Center, a medical clinic in Manhattan, New York. He is the co-founder of a boutique webhosting company, PeachyHost (http://www.peachyhost.com), and he loves helping non-techy people gain familiarity and comfort with the web world. When he is not working, Zach keeps active with biking, basketball, and tennis, and recently started working on a food blog with his girlfriend, Amanda—documenting the ways in which they make food work for a couple where one is vegetarian and the other enjoys meat (http://twocookscooking.com/). He hopes to one day open a restaurant and continue working with web, video, and audio.

What Big Whales, Smart Swifts, and Ambitious People Do (Move)

by Ronault LS (Polo) Catalani

*B*ecause our leaders back home—both imperial foreigners and bad local ones—did well by keeping us unschooled, our prose is an oral tradition. This djatung (story) is therefore written for rhythm and tone and phrasing as much as with vocabulary. Djatung are best read aloud in empty iron back stairways or tiled public restrooms. In bed with someone you love is good too.

Families move. We always have. Since memory began.

Humans move like Humpback whales move. Like arctic caribou, like Chapman Elementary's chimney swifts move. It's imprinted in cetacean ribs big as a school bus, in birdie bones light as a feather.

When whale families move, hushed Oregon State University scientists follow every breath blowing just above our cold Pacific's waves. Caribou migrating have inspired America's kindest conservationists to chill the world's biggest oilmen. Every September, hundreds of families on cozy blankets cheer Chapman Elementary's chimney swifts. Thousands and thousands spew out of that school's tall stack, chattering a mix of English and Spanish, eager to get down to sunnier Mexico. Bigger bugs too.

All ambitious families move across our earth's well-worn face. Take our President's pop, moving from Kisumu to Manoa for school; take Barack's mom moving him to Java for love; take him moving to LA then New York then Chicago then Washington DC, pretty baby girls in tow.

Our elder aunties have a saying back home, "Good boys and real men make their moms and wives proud. Only our lazy

and stupid sons stay in our poor kampong"—*in our village.*
That saying's moved with mi familia in an almost complete
circumnavigation of our marvelous blue marble.

We've all, always moved. And yet many of us are fonder of
moving fins and feathers than of other folk moving among us.

Portland's urban planners are easily the West's very best.
MAX, our tidy light rail leaves hardly a trace of carbon in its
swift wake. Our green-roofs carefully return rain to ground to
river to ocean. We revere River Columbia's cycles of Sockeye
and Steelhead. The intricate weave of our interdependent lives.
But not enough of us figure into our region's health our grand
circulatory system of human migration.

We move as naturally and perennially as all life moves. It's in
these bones. Borders are not.

Borders we declare by law. Borders we pencil on recyclable
paper.

Salem city limits used to determine where Black men could
not sleep at night. Multnomah County lines used to stop cold
Sheriff's boys in hot pursuit of bad guys. Oregon's border used
to map where Filipinos could marry white ladies, from where
we could not. Where Chinese could own laundries. Where white
men could own slaves.

While these jurisdictional lines faded, our national borders
hardened. Four generations of excluding and expelling families
migrating north, and folks steaming east, have left America oddly
homogenous. And mean.

And some of our leaders build futures as if us moving is different
from what swifts and salmon do. As if what drives families to do
what we have always done is distinct from what rain and rivers
and oceans have always done. In irresistible cycles. Naturally.

South to north. East to west. And then back again. Perennially.
Beautifully. Al'hamdulillaah.*

* Derived from Qor'anic Arabic, Al'hamdulillaah is Indo patois for
"All our grace is from God."

Andjing panas (hotdog)-on-a-stick

by Ronault LS (Polo) Catalani

Ogh. I've stayed plenty clear of *them*, down in that mall's cavernous foodcourt. I've done pretty good, ignoring them since they arrived. I'm not talking about those shrill Hong Kong girls, jabbing "Kung pao chicken! Kung pao chicken!" at startled lunchtime passers-by. I don't mean those anxious Korean kids poking toothpicked "Cajun chicken! Cajun chicken!" as if their young lives depended on it.

I'm talking about those thin expressionless Hotdog-on-a-Stick girls. All so-oh tall, in their vinyl go-go boots, wrapped in their striped tight tank tops and minis. Scar-ry.

I steer reeal wide, whenever I'm forced to pass their little booth, back basement corner, Pioneer Mall. They're not like you and me, no. Aliens, they are. I don't mean "alien," like Cambods or Kurds or Kosavars. These girls're from a whole other solar system. ETs in disguise.

There's always four or five of them, lanking around back there, chirping at each other.

Once, only once, I actually saw a customer approach their counter. He was fashionably casual. Eddie Bauer khakis and a sea mist polo, studying their menu. *Hotdog-on-a-Stick—$1.75 Fresh Lemonade—$1.75.*

They, three waxy white girls, closed in on Eddie, waiting for him to lower his eyes from their price list, waiting to snag his peepers. You never want to make eye contact with out-of-this-world types; Martian or layak or demonio—they'll put da juju on you, they'll drag you into their Hotdog-on-a-Stick backroom, and who knows, probably do all kinds of weird and wonderful exams, while your arms are velcroed to your sides, while you're lying naked as the day you were born. Aliens, they are. Interested in ev-ver-rything about us.

"NO EDDIE. Not so close!" I yelled (inside my head, mind you). And I was about to yank him back. But one of them—their tallest and slimmest, their blandest—looked up from her lemon squasher, looked up from under her brow and moving her perfectly paraffin lips ever so softly, mouthed: "Not ... a ... word, Earthling." I froze in my tracks.

"Will you be enjoying a Hotdog-on-a-Stick today, Sir?" their nearest looked Eddie up and down, up and down. I've seen that look before, *manu'u* stork standing statue-still in paddy rice, drawing in her long slender neck, measuring striking distance to an unsuspecting silvery minnow in her shadow.

Eddie moved on, not knowing how close to being lunch he was. He took a toothpick of two steaming chunks of kung pao chicken, he reached in his hip-pocket for a five buck bill. The Chinese chicks grinned. The alien girls glared. Two of them at their competitors. Two at me. I beat it.

Like I said, I stay plen-ty clear of *them*, down in their cavernous food court. That is, till last Saturday. While my baby did Victoria's Secret, I was doing my thing: baiting those teriyaki and Cajun girls, on my way to Cinnabon. They smell oh so good. Their buns.

That's when I noticed. That's when I let my eyes (startled, stupid) rest on that hotdog stand.

Five tall striped girls immediately made an erect semi-circle behind their tidy Sunkist lemons pyramids. And I knew right then, right there—in that white-lit backroom of their basement corner booth, those clever expeditionary commanders of Hotdog-on-a-Stick, had done their homework.

Out from between Hotdog-on-a-Stick girls Numbers 2 and 4, she stepped. She did. Their solution. To my avoidance. Their answer, to America's emerging demographics: Striped tank top and cap. Tall and slim. Cacao powder face and regulation almond eyes.

Dios mio, I whispered aloud, "our own eth-o-nick Hotdog-on-a-Stick girl." Awesome.

The cunning, the foresight, the marketing savvy. These guys

are good. As good as those Sunday sales page, kind'a Black, likely-Latina, maybe hapa-Haole chicas, in Mervyn's sun dresses and summer sandals. Beach-streak hair blowing. Great white shark grinning.

I approached her, mesmerized. Zombied, I was.

"Will you be enjoying a Hotdog-on-a-Stick today, *Kuya?*" she said, chocolate eyes checking me, up and down, up and down.

RONAULT LS (POLO) CATALANI
Polo's family was expelled from Indonesia, granted asylum in Netherlands, then resettled in Oregon. He's a West Coast and SE Asia activist-lawyer and a fellow of the International Court of Justice in The Hague. He is also contributing editor at *The Asian Reporter* and a commentator on Wisconsin, Milwaukie, and Oregon Public Radio. He wrote *Counter Culture: Immigrant Stories from Portland Café Counters*. Polo manages City Hall's New Portlander Programs.

Polo's daughter Caricia is a public health doctor; she teaches at UC Berkeley and researches in Indonesia and India. Artist son Aden has exhibited in Amsterdam, New York, Las Vegas, and San Francisco. Polo and artist wife Nim are new grandparents.

A Slanted View
by Simon Tam of *The Slants*

I play bass in what's often known as the first and only all-Asian American dance rock band in the world. We perform at many of the largest Asian cultural festivals in North America. We've been featured in and on over 1,500 radio stations, websites, magazines, and TV shows talking about the Asian American experience. My band members and I often facilitate workshops on cultural diversity, racism, and stereotypes about Asian and Asian American culture. In fact, when you look up information on the band, it's hard to find anything that doesn't associate us with Asian American culture, which is why when the U.S. Patent and Trademark Office (USPTO) said that our band's name was disparaging to persons of Asian descent, I was rather shocked.

The name that I and my cohort of pan-Asian Americans chose for the band is *The Slants*. We deliberately chose this outdated, generational term to inject pride into Asian American culture. Because of the broad support that we've had from Asian Pacific Americans (APAs), not only from media and blogs but also from lifelong activists who are aware of the sensitivities of the community-at-large, we never expected the USPTO to have an issue when we filed for a trademark on the band's name.

The Trademark Office doesn't allow terms that are deemed disparaging to be approved. In order for them to reject an application for a trademark on these grounds, they have to show that a substantial composite of the referenced group is offended by the word.

When we responded to the Trademark Office with evidence of support from the community, we included dozens of examples of Asian Pacific American media supporting our band. Well-known lifelong APA activists wrote letters of support for our use of the name. We also showed other examples of Asian Americans using the term "Slant" in a positive manner, such as the major APA Film Festival *Slant* and Chicago-based TV show *The Slant*.

So what kind of evidence did they bring to demonstrate the collected outrage of APAs who are offended by our name?

First, they cited UrbanDictionary.com. Then, they found an anonymous post on a message board from someone who said they didn't like our name. After that, they put in photographs of Miley Cyrus making a slant-eye gesture. They sent this to us along with a rejection letter that said the vast support we demonstrated from the APA community was "laudable" but not influential.

This is what angers me the most: the Trademark Office decided that anonymous wiki sources mattered more than the voice of Asian Americans. Why does a government agency that has no connection with APAs have the right to dictate what is appropriate for our community? Why don't we have the right to decide for ourselves?

Our plight reminds me of another case. You might know of the NFL team called the Washington *Redskins*. The litigation over their name has been going on since 1992 except in that case, the Trademark Office continues to defend their name despite formal objections, legal challenges, and lawsuits from Native Americans who find the term "Redskins" to be an offensive racial slur. Again, a government agency that has no connection with the referenced community is making decisions as to what is appropriate or offensive to them. In our case, they deny our trademark in the absence of any valid complaints from Asian Americans. With Native Americans, they continue to defend "Redskins" even in the face of formal objections.

The role of the government shouldn't include deciding what a group can define themselves as; that right should belong to the community itself. While I would love to win the trademark to protect my band's name—and frankly, to end the process because it's been a long and expensive one—this case is bigger than *The Slants*. This outcome will help determine what other minority groups are going to do in the future.

I've been accused by some that my work with *The Slants* is damaging and actually hurts the Asian American community because of our name. These are individuals who believe that the U.S. Patent and Trademark Office's decision was justified. Whether or not they believe that the government's role is to decide how communities can address themselves or not, these people feel that the term "slant" has not been and/or cannot be reclaimed by APAs. Not only does this affect our band, but it affects all APAs who are using the term "slant" in a positive, self-referential manner. This includes *Slant Film Festival*, popular Asian blogger *Slant Eye for the Round Eye*, *Slanted Magazine*, and numerous others. In a way, it also calls into question all of the APA media, organizations, and individuals that support us in our efforts as well.

I'm reminded of the words of Frank Wu, acclaimed Asian American author and Dean of the Wayne State Law School in Michigan, who eloquently wrote that, "If we are to make genuine progress toward racial justice, as opposed to rhetorical changes that celebrate differences in a shallow sense and create an elaborate etiquette of false sensitivity, we must be willing to consider claims about discrimination one by one rather than with assumptions. Some allegations of intolerance turn out to be true, even if not all of them have a basis in fact."

First, let's examine the idea that trademarking the name *The Slants* and/or my use of it is hurting the APA community. I can understand the rationale behind this thought: one might think that individuals would feel justified in referring to Asian Americans as "slants" and therefore disparage our community. I believe that if someone is going to be intentionally offensive, they are going to do it regardless of the labels at hand. If someone is going to be accidentally offensive (with no malicious feeling attached), it would be based on ignorance and not hate. Exposure to a term, "slant," when only used in a positive self-referential manner by members of our community is not going to propagate this. The re-appropriated term "gay" is one example. Someone can use it in a harmful manner or they can use it as a casual description because there is no sting left in the term on its own. Exposure to the notion that "slant" can actually be used as a term of pride by Asian Americans doesn't necessarily mean people are going to use it as a normative label (people are not forced to use the term). In fact, positive exposure helps the re-appropriation process because the way to fight ignorance is through education, not paying reverence to hate by fear of using the term.

The Slants have had some pretty significant exposure in the media. If you were to total the audience of our media coverage, it would exceed 25 million. We've appeared in 36 out of 50 states and have performed for audiences of over 10,000 on multiple occasions. We've always been connected with Asian American culture in a positive manner, both in the APA press as well as with media outside of our community. However, despite all of this attention, I have never encountered someone taking license to use the term "slant" with hostility and justifying its hateful use by citing our band. In fact, more often than not, we see APAs using the term with pride saying, "I have slanted eyes too. I'm proud of it!"

We are referring to our band as The Slants. It is ludicrous to believe that this would justify someone beginning to use the term in a hurtful manner as the common norm. A popular feminist magazine that also is named after a re-appropriated term, Bitch, isn't supporting people to call all females bitches. When Chinese rap artist Jin refers to himself as "chink" or "slant eye" in his lyrics, people aren't drawing the conclusion that they are justified in using the term. Constituents see that individuals directly tied to the referenced community are using it in a personal and positive manner. It is through positive exposure that we educate others on appropriate uses of a term as well as the necessity of bold acts of self-pride from members of under-represented communities.

There are some naysayers out there who don't believe in the power of re-appropriation or reclamation. Perhaps they doubt the power of the process for their own community specifically but accept it for others. However, the truth is that words and language can change throughout time (sometimes fairly quickly). A word on its own only contains as much power as we give it. The meaning can be positive and create a sense of pride, or it can be negative, depending on how it is used or how it is received.

Often times, we are using re-appropriated terms themselves but not even realizing it. For example, in referring to homosexuality the terms "gay" and "queer" were once pejoratives but now are socially acceptable terms to address the LGBTQ community. Other times we use terms that were once associated with race but since then have shed their associations with their original references (for example, "hooligan" was a disparaging term for the Irish; "hip hip hooray" used to be the rallying cry in 1819 Germany for killing Jews).

True, in the past, "slant" was occasionally used as a negative description for Asians. However, Asian American pioneers have reclaimed the term and the reality is that its contemporary usage is more commonly used in a positive self-referential manner than not. Somewhere along the line, Asians decided that having slanted eyes was not something to be ashamed of but, rather, something to be proud of. What was once used as something to oppress became something to boast about.

Some have argued that "slant" is like the "n-word" of the Asian race. I would argue that it is not. For one, the word slant has multiple meanings and connotations. With regards to its connection with Asians, it was simply a physical description. There was no emotional connection, whether positive or negative. Whereas some people (including many blacks) dislike saying *nigger* and are often times uncomfortable with even reading or writing the term, the same is not true of *slant*.

What race is a "slant" anyway? The term "slant eye" is a scientific description that comes from the term "palpebral slant" and can refer to any race because it describes the line from the inner eye to the outer. Often, it is associated with Asians since we generally have a more prominent palpebral slant than others.

Consider this: the 2001 first edition of the New Oxford American Dictionary contained multiple definitions for "slant." Among them was "DEROGATORY, a contemptuous term for an East Asian or Southeast Asian person." The 2005 edition read almost exactly the same, except it was updated to: "informal, offensive, a contemptuous term for an East Asian or Southeast

Asian person" ("DEROGATORY" label removed). Finally, the 2010 edition removed any associations with pejorative use.

In his work *Dictionaries: The Art and Craft of Lexicography*, lexicographer Sidney Landau (2001) points out that "How ... dictionary editors decide what to label offensive or disparaging ... is based on the editor's judgment of society's norms for the limits of reputable public behavior. He consults slang dictionaries and other written sources, including other general dictionaries"(p. 233).

I'm not arguing that it is impossible to find examples of people using the term "slant" in an offensive manner. The reality is that any ethnic, religious, or societal label can be used in a derogatory manner if the offense is clearly conveyed. But as one of the editors of the *New Oxford American Dictionary* states, "such a use is not evidence that the word itself is intrinsically disparaging or derogatory, or that the word itself will be received as offensive by the persons it is intended to describe."

When my mother refers to me as an "Oriental" because that was the term she learned when she entered the United States, I don't take offense to it. When someone blames our economy on "the Orientals in China," I do. I would feel flattered if someone said to me "I love the slant of your eyes," but I wouldn't if someone said, "You slants all look the same." I've even talked to some APAs who think that the word "Asian" can itself be offensive, because it is a blanket term that washes over hundreds of unique cultures, languages, histories, and ideas. The difference in reactions is rooted in intention and context. This is why the photograph of Miley Cyrus posing with a slant eye gesture was offensive: it was encouraging and legitimizing the taunting of APAs. There was no affection or pride contained within her actions.

Context matters. I believe that this is why we've had unilateral support from the Asian American media, bloggers, events, organizations, and individuals. This is why Asian Americans continue to support the *Slant Film Festival* (going on 10 years strong!), read the witty blogs at *Slant Eye for the Round Eye*, and support other APA artists who use the term in a positive manner.

It is because our community understands that before we judge someone, we should attempt to understand the context first.

Re-appropriating hateful terms in relation to race, culture, or religion can be an important part of the healing process for communities that have been disparaged. Even if one does not believe that this process is helpful, how can they argue that it is actually damaging? Perpetuating a hateful meaning is more hurtful towards the community than reclaiming it and injecting it with pride.

I can speak with experience on this. With our band, we have been successful at sharing our culture and APA perspectives with others who might not have had exposure to our world. This band has allowed me to travel across North America talking about race, stereotypes, and discrimination (I do roughly 20 workshops per year throughout the United States). Because of our name, we've been able to start conversations about race that might have never been had. I get letters every week from young Asian Americans thanking us for giving them an APA hero in the rock music scene (there aren't many) and making them "proud of their slanted eyes." I also get many notes from non-Asian Americans, thanking us for exposing them to our culture and countering stereotypes that have generally been assumed to be true.

Furthermore, the term isn't only being accepted by younger generations of APAs. We perform at APA festivals and events throughout the country for all ages. One community organizer recently told me that she enjoyed seeing the smiles of *Nisei* (Japanese elders) when watching our band at a local celebration. These were individuals who survived the WWII internment camps and were extremely pleased that we have created such strength in the community, rooting it in Asian American pride.

The Asian community has been using the term slant with pride for over a decade now and it has not divided or disparaged our community. In our generation, we've taken the hate out of the term. We've flooded the internet with our culture. Try searching for "slants" on Google and you'll find endless stories of an Asian band connected with Asian pride, Asian cultural festivals, and articles about APA issues. Through the work of APAs as a united community, we've literally changed the dictionary. And I can tell you that this slant is proud of it!

So let me wrap up by saying to the Asian American community: Thank you for your support over the years. Our love for spreading APA culture drives us to continue what we do. We're going to continue to fight ignorance with education, hate with love, negativity with positivity.

To the U.S. Trademark Office: Thank you for being offended on my behalf. You might not know this, but APAs have been a part of U.S. history since 1750, when Filipinos began settling here. We have helped build this country, from the railroads to shaping civil rights laws for all citizens. And believe it or not, we're grown-up enough now to decide what's right for ourselves. The broad, unified support of the Asian American community should be enough to trump that of UrbanDictionary.com (or at least the *New Oxford American Dictionary* should be more credible than a wiki-site). Our voice matters. You should listen, but then again, my view is a little "slanted."

SIMON TAM is a Chinese/Taiwanese American, an activist, and musician. He is the founder and bassist for *The Slants*, the first and only all Asian American dance rock band in the world. In addition to presenting a bold, unapologetic view of the API (Asian Pacific Islander) experience through his music, Simon also delivers workshops and talks on Asian American culture throughout the continent. He is an enthusiastic supporter of API advocacy organizations, adopting dogs, and fighting cancer.

An avid fan of music, reading, and diversity, Simon is a regular contributor to *API Crossroads* and *You Offend Me You Offend My Family*. His writing can be found at www.aslantedview.com. His band can be found at www.theslants.com

What a Difference a Word Makes
by Ben Efsanem

A recent article written by the musician Simon Tam outlined the struggles of his band and their ongoing battle with the U.S. Patent and Trademark Office to trademark the band's name. Their application has so far been denied on the grounds that the name of the band, *The Slants*, has been used historically to denigrate Asian people and, therefore, runs counter to the Trademark Office's policy of not permitting disparaging terms to be used.

According to Tam, the act of reclaiming or re-appropriating derogatory racist terms can be cathartic and may potentially "inject pride" into Asian American culture. It is also strongly suggested that this process might even diminish the offensiveness of anti-Asian slurs. The reasoning seems to be that the more a group uses a slur to describe themselves, the less power it has to offend them, therefore reducing the effectiveness of derogatory slurs and perhaps even giving the term a "positive" connotation. This concept is not new. Over the past thirty years, some elements within African American culture have undertaken to reclaim the N-word, using it as a self-referential term to such an extent that it is now extremely common to hear it being used in popular culture. Yet, can it be said that the N-word has lost its power to offend because it has become so ubiquitous? I do not believe that it has. Indeed, I think the very idea that racial slurs are simply terms of offense is a major category error that has the potential to diminish efforts to overcome prejudice.

The paradox of racist epithets is that, even though they reference racial characteristics in an abrasive or offensive manner, the aim is not to offend. To think of racist epithets in this way is naive because the goal has never been to bruise the egos of minorities, but rather to reinforce the idea of social and political inferiority by "putting them in their place." Understood in this way, it should become apparent that the notion that we can diminish the power of racial epithets through "re-appropriation" is actually absurd. This is because what's effectively being asserted is that one can de-institutionalize racism by adopting derogatory labels. The racial epithet is the symptom and casual expression of attitudes that see the minority group as inherently inferior, which in turn drives the creation and maintenance of institutions that maintain a social and political hierarchy based upon race.

In order to explain my argument, let me take a short tour through two millennia of Western philosophy, tradition, and civilization.

In the West, this concept of a racial hierarchy has deep roots that reach back to the very dawn of the philosophical traditions of Classical Greece. It was the ancient Greeks who first formulated the concept of themselves as an ideal race, whose climate and connection to the land made them especially suited to rule over the "lesser" races; their supposed physical and intellectual superiority meant this was the natural order. A common belief was that the climate and socio-political structure of Asia made the Asian into a meek follower who was feminine and spoiled. Although the ancient Greeks were referring mainly to the Persians (whom they considered to be Asiatic), later northern European proto-race scientists and thinkers of the 17th and 18th centuries adopted and perpetuated these attitudes and applied them to the whole of Asia. It is from them that ideas of racial superiority were updated and propagated into the modern world and became the basis for much of the racist horrors committed by Europe and America in subsequent centuries. It is thus a great irony that the Greeks viewed their northern European brethren as semi-intelligent man-beasts, adept at warfare, but intellectually feeble.

History lessons aside, the point of all this is that the attitudes that have driven the European and later the American desire to seek dominion over the "lesser" races are profoundly intertwined with their philosophical and historical heritage: it is who their culture says they are. The institutions that upheld slavery, indentured servitude, exclusion, and genocide rest on the assured knowledge that the European was created to rule—and the Asian to serve. This has been a fundamental aspect of Western thinking for well over two millennia.

From this perspective, it can be seen that the racist epithet is simply the basest expression of this philosophical tradition—a kind of racist philosophy for the common man, if you will. Calling someone a "slant" or a "gook" is an assertion of this philosophy of racial hierarchy, which means that to think of the epithet as a means to tease or wound the ego is an almost childlike conception. This would be tantamount to saying that the yellow star that the Jews were forced to wear in Nazi Germany was a mere insult. It was not. The yellow star signified that an individual belonged to a group that was deemed inferior and whose place in society was determined accordingly. For Asian Americans, our "yellow star" is our racial characteristics. What this means is that who we are or what we have the potential to be can be limited by the qualities that American culture has identified as typical of those who possess Asian racial characteristics. These qualities of "Asianness" are propagated through stereotyping and xenophobic political fear-mongering.

Perhaps it is becoming clear that anti-Asian epithets are more than simple derogatory references to eye shapes or their horizontal alignment on the face. If you possess Asian racial characteristics, then American culture propagates pre-set "truths" or beliefs about who you are and the type of character that you may have. These axioms will contribute to bamboo ceilings, salary inequalities, imbalances in representation in political or civic office, violence against your person, as well as the general attitude that Asians are not true Americans. By not recognizing the scope of anti-Asian epithets, those who promote their casual usage are effectively reinforcing their power. The reason is that by misunderstanding or misrepresenting the intent of the racial slur as a simple offensive term is to obscure the history of oppression, violence, and exclusion that they represent as well as the institutions of racism that they have been used to uphold.

So, what are the meanings of terms like "chinks," "gooks," "slants," or any of the other epithets that have been applied to Asian people? In short, they are terms of dehumanization. The original "chinks" and "slants" were the immigrant workers who came initially from China and later from other parts of East and Southeast Asia, and whose presence in America was resented and feared. The so-called chink was an interloper and invader whose racial differences inspired fear and loathing and whose willingness to work in the harshest conditions made him an economic threat to the social order. Only the most vehement hatred was reserved for the "chink" who, after all, was considered barely human. Violence against him was considered virtuous and justified. His rights to own property, to move freely, and to procreate were restricted. They were denied citizenship and basic human rights.

The "Chinatown" was thus created as a ghetto in which to concentrate the deplorable chink. There, he was harassed and attacked by police and citizen alike, whose violence against the early Asian immigrants was casual and routine. Concentrating the mainly male Asian immigrants in these "ethnic enclaves" also made it a convenient way to ensure that relationships and marriages with white women were easier to police and restrict. The Chinatown was effectively an attempt to limit the growth of Asian America through exclusion, with the ultimate aim of ethnically cleansing America of its Asian immigrants. So, in a word, being a "chink "or a "slant" meant persecution.

Even though very little of this history of brutality towards Asian people is remembered or even cared about by mainstream America, the power of the epithet to place Asian people in an inferior social and political position remains. It is no coincidence that American children of Asian descent who go through the US school system tend to report feelings of alienation, identity issues, and a sense of not belonging to American society. Given that the racial harassment and baiting of Asian children in American schools seems to be rampant and casual, this should come as no surprise. The power of the racial epithet to reinforce a social hierarchy is alive and well and is a part of the common experience for Asian American children.

Some people have asserted that this subject can be conceived of as a mere semantic issue. This argument suggests that words are not inherently offensive and can only hurt us in so much as we allow them to do so. This is a somewhat convoluted argument, which verges on sophistry. As I have already illustrated, the issue is not about offensiveness but the history that is obscured by trivializing the role that epithets have played in reinforcing a racist social order and ideology. A word cannot and should not hurt. What hurts is that the epithet and all of the attitudes that produce it can determine the tone, quality, and even the direction of our lives. Even if one succeeds in defusing the offensiveness of the slur, the prejudice that creates it will remain. So yes, while it is true that words in their pure form may not be demeaning, this is ultimately a meaningless argument because it is social and political inequality that enables such words to have power.

What this means is that derogatory epithets do not lose power because we might "own" them or use them to describe ourselves. They lose power when the structures that enable a given group to utilize them as a means to reinforce ideas of social, racial, and political superiority over another group are dismantled or are themselves disempowered. This is why the N-word can be said to be reclaimed and owned. Although it still causes offense, it can no longer be used with impunity because the structures that empowered it have been or are in the process of being dismantled. A huge part of this process is the understanding and common acceptance that usage of the N-word by white America was representative of a history of brutality, violence, and slavery. You might well notice that many white Americans are visibly embarrassed and uncomfortable when they hear the N-word and might even try to disassociate themselves from its use. This is because the term is associated with slavery, rape, murder, and inhumanity. No one wants to associate themselves with the connotations of its use.

The Asian community is not there yet. Anti-Asian racial slurs are trivialized and, for the most part, they can be or often are used casually and without social repercussion. This was illustrated in the outpourings of racist vindictiveness following the recent earthquake and tsunami that struck Japan; hostile attitudes towards Asian people lie very close to the surface of mainstream American consciousness. The individuals whose anti-Japanese fervor was expressed on various social networking sites with mockery and epithets did not belong to marginalized extremist organizations. They were average, everyday Americans openly and unashamedly displaying their hostility.[1] This tells me that we need to strive harder to bring to consciousness the racist ideological basis of anti-Asian epithets and stereotyping, instead of trivializing the issue by characterizing it as childish name-calling. America should feel shame and discomfort that it has and continues to use racist epithets to reinforce the inferiority of Asian Americans. That would be a true measure of success for any Asian activism.

To summarize, racial epithets are not intended to offend. Their purpose is to assert ideas about the social, political, or racial inferiority of the target group. Thinking of them as merely offensive words is to obscure this fact. Epithets reflect an ideology of dehumanization that has been the foundation of many of history's atrocities. Applied to Asian people, the epithet reminds us of our status as outsiders and interlopers who can never quite be true Americans. The anti-Asian epithets reflect the fantasy of America, as reflected in its popular culture, that violence towards the Asian—particularly the Asian man—is easily justified and is almost virtuous. The epithet reminds us that America attempted to ethnically cleanse its nation of the early Asian immigrants, and its popular culture still exhibits fantasies of the mass killing of Asians. There is nothing trivial about the racist epithet. This is why I cannot support a movement whose aim is to persuade a government agency that an anti-Asian epithet is little more than a term of offense. We should be striving to do the opposite and show how the racist epithet is a reflection and reinforcement of deep-rooted prejudice and institutional oppression.

Terms like "slant" and "chink" should never have positive connotations; this obscures the history and suffering of the earliest Asian immigrants. We should always remind society that, for the people to whom they were applied, these terms reflected suffering, degradation, hatred, and brutality. This fact should never be obscured. To do so would be like trying to give terms like "Nazi" or "holocaust" some positive connotations. America is already comfortably and even willfully ignorant of its historical prejudice towards Asians—the repercussions of which are still experienced in the present day.

On a final note, it is only fair to acknowledge that Simon Tam and his band are activists and do strive to bring to light the experiences of Asian Americans. For this, they should be applauded. I believe, however, that they are undermining their own activism by pursuing this goal of trivializing racist epithets. I personally see little evidence that re-appropriating a derogatory term promotes cultural pride or social empowerment and believe that successful advocacy must be based on a solid and accurate understanding of the nature of our experiences.

NOTES

[1]See the following websites for examples:

http://disgrasian.com/2011/03/disgrasian-of-the-weak-bigotry-n-japan-post-tsunami/

http://colorlines.com/archives/2011/03/whats_with_the_post-earthquake_anti-japanese_animus.html

http://blog.angryasianman.com/2011/03/hey-you-fking-facebook-idiots-japanese.html

http://www.japanprobe.com/2011/03/14/paul-watson-tsunami-that-killed-hundreds-of-japanese-was-divine-punishment/

BEN EFSANEM considers himself a nomadic soul. Born in Asia, raised mostly in Europe, and married in America, he now lives with his family in Istanbul, Turkey, where he eats a lot of kebabs. He takes a keen interest in Asian-American issues and sees the development of an autonomous Asian-American culture and worldview as key to the progress of the community. His other interests include food, wine, and music. He completed an art degree in England and uses his skills to paint for pleasure. Ben blogs under Ben Efsaneyim at http://benefsanem.blogspot.com.

Two Letters from My Lost Father:
A Transracial Adoptee Shares His Heart
by Koh Mo Il (Nicholas D. Hartlep)

Who Will Love My Children (1983) was a made-for-television movie about a real woman, Lucile Frey. In 1952—upon the birth of her tenth child—Mrs. Frey, a poor, semi-educated, White rural Iowa mother, learns that she will ultimately die of cancer. Anticipating that her husband will not be able to take care of their children on his own, Frey takes it as her job to find suitable foster parents for her "soon-to-be" orphaned children. Before the emotional film ends, viewers learn that the Frey children were able to retain their familial ties, despite being separated for 29 years. In fact, the actual Frey children were showcased the same evening that *Who Will Love My Children* premiered (February 15, 1983) on an installment of the ABC TV series *That's Incredible* (O'Connor, 1983). I learned about this film in a sermon that my pastor gave. The pastor shared that he was adopted and that he had watched the film and it caused him to adopt his youngest son.

I don't find it *incredible* that the life story of a White woman from Iowa would be publicized instead of a woman of color's life like that of a Korean woman's given that the Asian American community continues to be a marginalized sector of society. I do find it *incredible*, though, that Asian Americans generally, and adopted Asian Americans particularly, continue to be an overlooked population. Unless the attention is "model minority" related—showcasing how Asian Americans are academically successful—Asian Americans receive little to no attention. For instance, Vincent Chin was a Chinese American adoptee, yet people talk mostly about his grisly death, not that he was a murdered member of the Asian American adoptee family (e.g., see Chang, 1999). I reference the storyline of the film *Who Will Love My Children* because it intersects similarly with my own adoption story quite well.

Who Loves Me?: My First Letter from My Lost Father
I learned that my biological parents' decision to give me up for adoption came shortly after my biological mother, Bang Ok Joo, was informed that she was going to die from cancer (which she succumbed to before my first year of life). Similar to Mrs. Frey's situation in *Who Will Love My Children*, my biological father, Koh Bong Joon, was not able to care for me without my mother and reluctantly chose to give me up for adoption. I say *reluctantly*, because on March 29, 2011, with the help of Children's Home Society and Family Services (CHSFS), I located my biological father in Korea. The first letter that I received from my birth father clearly conveys his hesitancy, shame, and the eventual misery that accompanied the decision to give me up for adoption:

To Nicholas Hartlep
[written in English verbatim from original text]
Trusting that you will understand this good-for-nothing father who confesses his great sin to his son and to God, I put forward the courage and start this letter. I am sorry. I beg for forgiveness. At the time I sent you [for adoption], your birthmother, due to an illness, gone to heaven first (cancer) raised you for one year and I had the minister come and we had a service for your first birthday. I couldn't raise you by myself. On one day in the winter when the snow was falling, I sent you to an unknown world. Every time I thought of you, I missed you, cried and have been trapped in my overwhelming guilt. I wandered aimlessly. I tried to die, but was rescued just in time.

Those were difficult times. Then in 1986, I met my present wife and began to study seminary and in March of 1998, I was ordained as a minister. I am doing God's work now. My wife and I have a son [named] Samuel Ko [born in 1987] and he is a freshman at Kyungmin University. He is preparing to be a chef. My wife was born in 1959 and I am Ko Bong Jun and was born in 1957. My hometown is Korea's Jeju Island. Now I live in Seoul in Sanggye-dong.

I am truly sorry. I lived so long with such deep sadness and tears. When I think of you, my son, it feels like my heart is going to rip and the pain makes me cry. Even now, I shed tears as I write this letter. This is all my fault. However, when I see how upstanding, strong, and sincere you have grown and matured, I am so very grateful. Since this good-for-nothing father of yours began to believe in Jesus Christ and started to pray, I have prayed for you. I prayed in earnest that wherever you live, wherever you are, God would protect you in His love and blessings. I deliberately have witnessed the blessing of the Lord to those isolated and in difficult positions in their lives—those in juvenile detention centers, prisons, and those in hospitals for patients with pulmonary tuberculosis. However, my own son, during all the time I've been doing this, has been having his own difficult time contending with a difficult environment of his own blood and tears in the United States. I am so sorry. But now there will be only good days ahead. That's because we have a dream. In doing God's work, I have been to Los Angeles in the United States 3 times, Hawaii 2 times, to Japan 17 times, etc. I have been diligently working as a missionary. My visa that allows me to go to the United States is good until 2015; it is a 10-year visa and has B1 and B2 visas.

I have put the explanations of the photographs on the back of them. There are pictures of my wife, my two sons, and also of my mission work. Let's pray for the two of us to meet. I am grateful to you, my son and to my daughter-in-law, your wife. I want to see cute, pretty Hye Jin and Ha Na as soon as possible. I am prepared to meet you anytime. And going into this with the mind of "Son, please forgive me," I am would like to talk with you about my failure to fulfill the role of father to you. And I am so extremely grateful that you are a Christian who believes in the same

Jesus that I serve.
Let's pray for each other. Thank you. I am sorry.
I love you.
In Korea, from your good-for-nothing father
March 27, 2011
Ko, Bong Jun

My Korean father was so excited and grateful that I searched for him. I began the search for my biological parents in January of 2011. This process began with me penning a letter to them, which they would read if the Korean investigators found either one of them in Korea. My letter is below.

Dear Mom and Dad,
My life has been difficult. I have been caught in between two worlds: the world I know here in the United States and the world that I want to know, that in South Korea. I am married and have two children of my own. My wife is Stacey, she is a nurse at a children's hospital. Our oldest daughter, Chloe, is three years old, while our youngest, Avery is 1 year old. Chloe's middle name is Korean, Haejin while Avery's is also Korean, Hana. I have always wanted to find out more about you both (my biological parents). The hardest thing about writing this letter is that it may be read and disregarded. I do not fully understand Korean culture, how would I? I was raised by two White Americans. As people tell me, you cannot teach something that you do not know. In November, I celebrated my 27th birthday. I am currently finishing my Ph.D. in Urban Education. I study at the University of Wisconsin-Milwaukee. I am a passionate scholar and try to stress education to my children. I wish to be a professor of education when I graduate.
I am an avid runner and enjoy the outdoors. I have read files in my adoption folder. I would say that I am still "stubborn" but I am a born-again Christian. From what I have read and studied about Korean and Asian (e.g. Chinese, Japanese) societies, Christianity is a minority religion. Do

you abide by Confucianism? In many ways I try to live a life of self-asceticism … perhaps for different reasons than Confucius, but similar nonetheless. With this letter I have included pictures of me, my wife, and my two children. Please keep them, it means a lot to me if you keep them. I would like to see a picture of you both. I do not have, at least to my knowledge, a single photograph of either of you.

My adoption has been a hard thing to deal with in my life. I wish I was with you both since I am a Korean by blood. Everyone tells me that by coming to the United States my life is better than it would be in Korea. However, how would these people know? I think this is the American modus Vivendi: "We know best." Truthfully, I am—more than my wife—interested in adopting a Korean child. It sounds contradictory, but I want to raise an adoptee since I know what it feels like being adopted. Oftentimes I feel like an orphan. I feel like it is me against the world. Besides my wife, I do not fully believe anyone loves or cares about me. My adoptive parents divorced when I was around 8 years old. I internalized their break-up and thought that their break-up was my fault. This has led me to attempt to be a perfectionist. Society here in America believes that all Asians are successful. The phrase for this is "model minority." My neighbor is a Korean man who was adopted from Seoul when he was young, too. Was my conception a taboo or a bad thing in Korean culture? I do not want you to forget me: please do not be afraid to take a stand and to get to know me. If you do not wish to meet me or communicate with me is your prerogative; but please know that if you choose to not speak or write me that you will be injuring me more.

I have goose bumps writing this letter. I do not know the outcomes that are to come, yet I am hopeful that someday we can know one another more than we do at the present time. If there are specifics or particular things you would like to know about me, please write me back. I was told that any letters sent and received will be translated. I want

*to learn Korean and Hangul. I speak Spanish and English.
I have traveled to many European countries and Ecuador,
South America as well. Someday I wish to return to my
natal country, South Korea. Have you ever traveled outside
of South Korea? I hope to hear from you soon. If not,
please keep this letter as a remembrance of the son you
never knew.
Nicholas D. Hartlep*

June 29, 2011 was the day that I learned that my biological
father booked a flight to visit me in Minneapolis (St. Paul),
Minnesota. As I write this essay, I have not met him, since he
is scheduled to arrive at the Minneapolis Airport on September
16, 2011. Notwithstanding, my birth parent search has been an
empowering experience for me.

Life's Two Defining Moments:
I am Not White and Racial Bullying

I am Not White

As a transracial adoptee, there are two defining moments for
me. The first is the moment that I realized that I was not White,
and the second is being bullied relentlessly in school. I became
consciously aware that I was an adopted child during the time
that my adoptive parents were going through a messy divorce.
Their divorce was "messy" to me because as an eight-year-old
child, I had a difficult time understanding why and how I would
have a "stepfather," and why and how I would have to visit
my adoptive "father." As a young boy, the whole situation and
impending scenario seemed unfair to me on so many levels.

Moreover, now as a married man, it is difficult for me to fully
grasp the reason(s) why my adoptive parents divorced—especially
since my wife and I believe that matrimony is "for better" or "for
worse" and that husbands and wives are supposed to marry their
soul mate, someone that they so deeply love that they do not
want to spend the rest of their life without them. When I was a
child, I thought it seemed unnatural to "fall out of love" with

one's spouse, and that is how it still feels to me. Adding salt to my wounds, I later learned that my adoptive mother was married before my father, but was quickly divorced.

The fact that I realized that I was non-White during my parents' divorce is normal and maybe even to be expected. Research and literature support the belief that divorces are difficult experiences for children. Divorces may be one "trigger event" that will elicit a focus on being adopted. I remember clearly the day that my adoptive mother told me that she was not going to stay married to my adoptive father. I was in the laundry room; I remember it well. A flood of thoughts and hurts entered my mind, body, and spirit at that exact moment. I told my mother that I would never accept another father (a "stepfather"). I cried a lot, and I was extremely angry and felt broken inside. Reflecting on this whole ordeal as an adult, I can safely say that I experienced all of Elisabeth Kübler-Ross' five stages of grief: denial, anger, bargaining, depression, and finally acceptance.

During my adoptive parents' divorce, I remember repeating and rehearsing in my mind that my parents were not really getting divorced—*denial*. This was followed by being *angry* at Jim (my soon-to-be stepfather), whom I believed was a marriage-wrecker. I also recall making compromises in my mind that my mom would be happier and that my dad could always remarry (which he eventually did)—*bargaining*. I was *depressed* during middle and high school, and I do not know when I finally *accepted* their divorce (perhaps I am still at a stage of ambivalence).

Racial Bullying

This time of divorce coincides with several racial or existential experiences that I had while I was a public school student. I attended an elementary school in West DePere, Wisconsin. The school, like its community, was majority White. While in school during this time, I remember being called racist epithets. I recall walking home from school one afternoon and being called a "chink" by two White students. This was the first time I consciously remember being hurt and wounded by a racist invective. Research documents the racism adopted Asian Americans endure in schools (e.g., see Chou & Feagin, 2010). There is a subtle undercurrent of racism in schools and society (e.g., see Hartlep, 2010).

When I returned home that particular day, I stared at the family photo that I had passed by so many other times. This time was different though. This family portrait was placed on the hearth of the fireplace in our family room. It showed all of my family members at that time—my adoptive mother, Sue, my adoptive father, Mike, and my sister, Lindsay (also an adopted Korean). I stood at the hearth while looking at the family photograph. I was transfixed by the people and their faces and hair. Why did my sister and I have black hair while my parents had blonde and brown hair? Why did my sister's and my eyes slant like almonds? It was during that moment that I felt I did not belong. It was then that I realized that I was not White. I had to know more, but I did not know what.

Looking back at that moment, I guess I was unconscious of my race and where I fit into society at large. After my racial and familial epiphany, I certainly had my doubts about calling my adoptive parents "mom" or "dad." Who was I? I asked my mother if I was her "real" son, and she assured me that I was. However, I was not so easily convinced. If I was her son, why did I not look like her or my father? My mother explained that I was adopted. It was hard for me to understand this process, other than the "common story" she told me. You know, "your parents loved you dearly, but knew you would have a better life in America. They wanted what was best for you, so they decided to give you up for adoption." The examples I have just given are far from the exception; they are the norm for Asian Americans and Asian American adoptees. These events and stresses wear thin on Asian Americans and even motivate many men and women to go under the knife and have surgeries such as breast implants or eye-lid surgery (e.g., see Chen & Yoo, 2010a, 2010b).

My adoptive mother told me that although my birth parents in Korea cared for me, they could not take care of me. They loved me so much that they decided it was best for me to be put up for adoption. In her own mind, my adoptive mother's rationale and the gist of her account of my adoption were ones of sincerity and love. However, reflecting on my questioning session, and also my life heretofore, I do not think it in the best interest of anyone to "sugar-coat" an adoption story. Why? Because an adoption story is a story of the adoptee and his/her parents, not the adopter(s) (e.g., see Dorrow, 1999; Han, 2010; Hartlep, 2011).

For instance, if I were not called a "chink" and "gook" that fateful day when I was in elementary school walking home from school, would I have ever realized that I was not White? Perhaps I would eventually, but this begs the question, should I identify as a Korean, American, or Korean-American? I have never liked the hyphenated American names. I consider myself as Korean. Other than my phenotypical traits, however, I am as American as they come. I grew up being socialized by two White parents, have had relatively few Korean friends growing up, and know very little of Korean culture.

Racism without Racists: Colorblind Families

My parents' divorce, my adoption, and my personal experiences with racism in school and society further cement the idea in my head that the majority of "Americans" and adoptive families do not know how racist the world is (e.g., see Bonilla-Silva, 2010; Hartlep, 2010, 2011). This idea has been coined "racism without racists" by Eduardo Bonilla-Silva (2010). According to Bonilla-Silva (2010, p. 29, italics added), "Color-blind racism is *racism without racists!*" Since many people—including adoptive parents—believe that colorblindness is neither racist in intent nor effect, transracial adoptive families rarely discuss the topic of racism with their child(ren). Therefore having a dialogue about racism becomes taboo and is avoided at all costs. Sara Docan-Morgan (2011) informs her readers that "race and racism are often viewed as *socially inappropriate* topics for discussion, particularly by White people [and adoptive families]" (p. 340, italics in original).

My parents, Sue and Mike, adopted me from Seoul, South Korea, when I was 13 months old. It is odd, until I began writing this essay, I would always tell people who asked me how old I was when I was adopted that I was 18 months old. Sometimes

I would say 2 years old and other times I would say 1 year old. My responses were based on how I felt. To me, my adoption story was a mythical thing and I got to set the parameters. Why shouldn't I? These questioners would never know if I was telling them the truth, and many times I do not think they even wanted to hear the truth or even cared. Why would I say this? Because they only wanted to make "small talk." I would hear comments like, "Aren't you so glad that you were brought to America? Now you have so much more opportunity." Many of the comments I received would be very *status quo* and very ethnocentric. Truth-be-told, I do not know if I am glad I was adopted. You see, adoptees must grapple with deep life questions. These questions include, what is my identity and who is my family? How do I best fit in? Is assimilation the best way to become an insider, or should I retain something of my heritage identity?

Many times people discuss the idea of "nature" vs. "nurture"— getting at the idea that individuals may be born with "such-and-such" disposition—while others argue that individuals are socialized to have "such-and-such" disposition. I contend that "nurture" or "socialization" is the most prominent process in children's lives. I may have been born in Korea, but I was raised in America by two White Americans. If I were not exposed to Korean culture, ways of living, beliefs, and practices, then Korea would remain unimportant in my life. John Palmer (2011) refers to this as being racially Asian but culturally White.

Empowerment through Writing: I am a Writer

For this reason, in many ways I am writing this essay as a form of catharsis. By writing down my thoughts, I begin to gain a sense of who I really am. Through this process of writing, I am empowered and begin to realize that I am unique and that many can learn from my experiences. When my adoptive parents learned of my decision to conduct a birth parent search, they were less than enthusiastic. I recall remarks my adoptive father, who possessed some paperwork on my adoption, made. He told me that he would like the original documents back when I was done using them for this research. How odd, I thought. If I never asked him to see my files, he would not have thought about them. How long had these files sat in his file cabinet, never looked at, only collecting dust? How many times did he ever read and review them? When I explained all of this to my dad, he only replied that they were "special" to him. If special means never thinking about or using something, then I agree with him that they must be special. My adoptive mother's only response was that she always knew deep down in her heart that someday I would try and find my birth parents. How she would know this is beyond me.

Many things struck me when I was reviewing my adoption papers. The first is how clueless my adoptive parents were when they adopted me. They were not required to learn about Korean culture. Why did they not even go to Korea to pick me up? I have a step-niece (Jennifer) who is adopted from Guatemala, and her two adoptive parents were obligated to go to Guatemala for two weeks and to promise to maintain Jennifer's heritage language (Spanish) during her childhood in America. What a difference that would have made in my own life if my parents were required to learn Korean and to maintain my heritage language.

The second thing that struck me was that my adoptive father inadvertently misspelled my Korean name on my paperwork filing for my Social Security number and naturalization. On the application he wrote that my name was Mo Il Kohl instead of the correct spelling, Mo Il Koh. This is not small potatoes. What would happen if someone had spelled my wife's name "Stacy," when in fact it is spelled "Stacey," on her social security card application? Misspellings of names are a huge deal. How would a college graduate like it if his/her diploma read a name that was spelled incorrectly? I suppose s/he would like to have the mistake corrected. I have a better example of the importance of names and spelling. A prominent researcher I work with received a certificate from President Obama. On her certificate, her name was spelled incorrectly. She asked whether or not she should request that the White House reprint her certificate. I and a host of her other colleagues answered in the affirmative: yes! What I am trying to say is that my adoptive parents knew very little about Korea and the culture that I would have been raised in. If they knew anything about Korean surnames, they would know that Kohl is not a Korean last name, rather Koh is. To me, adoptions and scenarios like mine are not idyllic—this is why there should be no "sugar-coating." Adoptions are many times assimilationist, whereby the adopted child gives up the life he would have had, for a life only his/her parents know.

The third thing that caught my attention was that my biological mother was a young mother. She was 23 years old when she had me; my biological father was 27 years old. At the time of writing this essay I am 27 years old, and my wife Stacey was 23 years old when she had our first daughter, Chloe Haejin. Being a young parent is difficult—this I know. My wife and I were not married when we conceived Haejin, but we were married before she was born. My biological parents were not married when they conceived me, but I believe they had intentions to do so. This is where it is difficult for me to fully understand the Korean culture. My adoption case worker, Tanya (a pseudonym), told me that the Korean culture is one in which, if a woman is not married and gives birth to a child, it is looked down upon. Therefore, having a child out of wedlock must certainly have presented Bang Ok Joo and Koh Bong Joon difficulties. My mother Bang Ok Joo, who was blind in one eye, was an elementary school graduate while my father Koh Bong Joon was a middle school graduate. As I mentioned in the beginning of this essay, my biological mother died of cancer. This is a large reason why I was placed for adoption. However, my biological parents' situation was drastically different than that of Stacey and me: Stacey graduated with her bachelor's degree before Chloe was born, and so did I. We had education on our side, and education is important since it helps determine one's income.

Who Loves Me?: My Second Letter from My Lost Father

I want readers of this *Thymos* anthology to understand that being an Asian American in the twenty-first century means that you often feel invisible, alone, and hurt. Many perceive that I am an "angry adoptee" (Palmer, 2011). While this may describe me in certain instances, I believe I am much more than angry. I am a son, a husband, a family member, a father, and according to my Christian faith, a son of God. I find it reprehensible that Asian Americans' lives and stories continue to be marginalized; this is what makes me angry. I hope that my true and painful story brings hope to yours, especially if you are an Asian American; for if there is no hope, we are already dead. The second letter (July 27, 2011) from my lost but found father concludes this essay. The letter illustrates the great love my father has for me and the new beginnings he wishes to make with me. I am forever grateful that like in the film *Who Will Love My Children*, I will get to have a family reunion with my father.

Received July 27, 2011

To my son whom I love and want to see:
When I first read your letter that said you forgive this good-for-nothing father [me], I was so overwhelmed and at a loss; I wept for a long time. It was like the same happiness and gratitude as when I first repented and received the forgiveness from meeting Jesus. It was that much of an impressive, great feeling.

I became a pastor and over the past 20 years, about 1200 times I have relayed the gospel to inmates nationwide in Korea. And I cannot deny the ▮▮▮▮ and providence of God that has made me the trumpet of his gospel conveying the Lord's love throughout the world—five times as revival lecturer in the United States, 17 times in Japan, and about 25 churches as a lecturer in China twice, Uzbekistan, Sri Lanka, Indonesia, Pakistan, Thailand, etc.

After having set away [for adoption] the son whom I love for a long time I wobbled and was in pain—in such pain that I tried twice to commit suicide. During that time, but the grace of God, I met my present wife and received her guidance. While living together in our beliefs with my wife's active prayer and via her help and love, I prayed during the day and I graduated from night school seminary, from graduate school and then in March 1998 was ordained as a minister. That was the grace of the Lord and the complete love of my wife. However, more than anything else, when I think of not having any resolution to the guilt and apology I felt regarding you and then lamenting in front of Jesus and deeply entering my belief [in the Lord], I wonder if it was that which provided you, Mo Il, the motive to become a minister.

My son [you] is writing his dissertation and this father [I] pray that the Lord will give you the wisdom he gave King Solomon, so certainly if you pray as you write, I believe that you will write a wonderful dissertation.

Your birthmother had lung cancer and was cremated. I boarded a ferry headed for my hometown of Jeju Island and spread her ashes in the ocean. I incinerated all photographs, so there is no trace [of her]. Let's forget all of our sad talk. I mean let's bury it in our hearts and be rid of it. I now know your email address and I have visited your website, so [I see] you've written a book! You resemble your grandfather. Grandfather was a poet and was a teacher who wrote sijo well. He was a teacher of Chinese characters and he had many students. It seems you have inherited the talent for writing. I have no relatives. I am the fourth generation of only sons. In this family, sons are very rare. However, I have become the Lord's laborer and am led by the many family members in Heaven.

In my heart, I want to fly to America immediately, but I am very much taking note of the fact that it seems you should come first to this motherland of yours that you so very much miss. But when my son receives his Ph.D., I would like to go to America and give you all at once, all the congratulations that I have not been able to give you. The place you were born is in Seoul in Nowon-gu's Kongneung-dong [Gongneung-dong]. I live in that same place Nowon-gu and I live in Sangye-dong there. If you come to Seoul, I [would like you to see] the palaces in Seoul, Namsan, evening tour of Seoul downtown and Gyeonggi-do Yongin's Folk Village and it is just a 50-minute domestic flight to Jeju/

Cheju Island which is my hometown. My email address is ▨▨▨▨▨▨▨▨▨▨▨. I have Googled and gone into your website and seen the tremendous amounts of information there (videos, theses, articles, etc.) I'm so proud! You are amazing. Just as I thought, my son is certainly someone of whom to be proud.

Well, I guess I'm most curious as to when you will come to Korea for the first time. I hope when you come, you do not come alone, but rather come with your whole family. And I need to know the days you will be in Korea, so I can make the travel [sightseeing] plans accordingly. And you should sleep in the house in which I live for 1-2 nights, I hope, as well and get closer to your two younger siblings. Koh Samuel is in his fourth year at seminary and he is in charge of married couples leadership, so this June 24, he will go on a graduation trip to "Kyushu," Japan for two nights and three days.

My passion is only Jesus. I have been invited from places around the world and have run there as lecturer about 500 times, and prison mission work about 1200 times, but my goal is 3000 times as part of the vision I have. Now that I have met you, my son Mo Il, now it seems my passion will be praying that [the Lord gives you what you need for] you to become an amazing Christian Ph.D., a professor, a father, a husband, and the working pillar of your church, and my loving son who is respected by many. I so want to see you quickly [as soon as possible] … I mean [I want to see] my son whom I love and who has grown up so wonderfully. The name Mo Il means to become the only such wonderful son in the world. I want to see you right away. I pray in the name of Jesus that you, my daughter-in-law and my two grandchildren, all whom I love, will be filled with the great grace and love of the Lord …

In Seoul, Korea
Written by Father to my son whom I love
June 7, 2011

*This is a streaming video of when I was invited as an instructor/presenter at an all-night youth ministries worship (Poo Nyu Mah Mission) at Yoido Full Gospel Church's Sanctuary of the Disciple Paul.
* I saw your video on YouTube. It was too bad that it was so short. It would be good if you put several together and made it about 10 minutes long. It's so good to be able to see your face and hear your voice [via this video]. Until we meet, this will comfort my heart. I love you.

REFERENCES

Bonilla-Silva, E. (2010). *Racism without racists: Color-blind racism & racial inequality in contemporary America* (3rd ed.). Lanham, MD: Rowman & Littlefield.

Chang, R. S. (1999). *Disoriented: Asian Americans, Law, and the Nation State.* New York, NY: New York University Press.

Chen, E., & Yoo, G. J. (Eds.) (2010a). *Encyclopedia of Asian American issues today: Volume 1.* Santa Barbara, CA: ABC-CLIO.

Chen, E., & Yoo, G. J. (Eds.) (2010b). *Encyclopedia of Asian American issues today: Volume 2.* Santa Barbara, CA: ABC-CLIO.

Chou, R. S., & Feagin, J. (2010). *The myth of the model minority: Asian Americans facing racism.* Boulder, CO: Paradigm.

Docan-Morgan, S. (2011). "They don't know what it's like to be in my shoes": Topic avoidance about race in transracially adoptive families. *Journal of Social and Personal Relationships, 28*(3), 336–355.

Dorrow, S. (Ed.) (1999). *I wish for you a beautiful life: Letters from the Korean birth mothers of Ae Ran Won to their children.* St. Paul, MN: Yeong and Yeong Book Company.

Han, S. (Ed.) (2010). *Dreaming of a world: Korean birth mothers tell their stories.* St. Paul, MN: Yeong and Yeong Book Company.

Hartlep, N. D. (2010). *Going public: Critical race theory and issues of social justice.* Mustang, OK: Tate Publishing.

Hartlep, N. D. (2011). Cultural Citizenship, not Color-Blindness: A Korean Adoptee's Plea to Parents. *Korean Quarterly, 14*(4), 18.

O'Connor, J. J. (1983, February 14). TV: Ann-Margret Plays a Dying Mother of 10. *The New York Times*. Retrieved on August 21, 2011 from http://www.nytimes.com/1983/02/14/arts/tv-ann-margret-plays-a-dying-mother-of-10.html

Palmer, J. D. (2011). *The Dance of Identities: Korean Adoptees and Their Journey toward Empowerment*. Honolulu, HI: University of Hawaii Press.

NICHOLAS D. HARTLEP is an advanced opportunity program fellow and Ph.D. candidate in the Urban Education Doctoral Program at the University of Wisconsin-Milwaukee. His latest book is *Going Public: Critical Race Theory and Issues of Social Justice* (2010). He can be contacted via email: nhartlep@uwm.edu or via his website www.hartlep.tateauthor.com

The Beekeeper
by Tony Robles

He walked in with a belt
Equipped with mace, a taser,
Handcuffs and, upon closer
Inspection, a can of what
Appeared to be Van Camps
Pork and beans

I was the new guy on his
First day of work as a security
Officer at a supermarket
In the barrio

I was to receive my training
On my responsibilities as
A security guard from
This man

I looked at the taser,
(Also known as a non-lethal
electronic stun gun)
It looked like a .45

He said he had
Caught a woman stealing
Roasted herb chicken
The day before

Told me he had special
Friends on the police force

And that he played golf and
Went to their houses for dinner

He said he was involved in
Clandestine governmental
Operations that he couldn't
Discuss (Of course)

We stood and watched people
Select food laden with
Sodium and fat

He told me that my job was
To be a visual deterrent
To shoplifting

Occasionally a female
Would walk by and he would
Remark under his breath
Nice ass
He said he was a
Bee keeper in his
Spare time, knew everything
There was to know about bees

Said that bees don't like
The color black
For some reason

A few minutes later this
African Descended guy I knew
Walked in wearing a yellow
Rain suit

It was raining and Ernie
Was black, dark honey
Chocolate black and looking

Like a 5 foot 10 inch bee

We stood and the guy with
The taser then told me
Of a kidney problem he
Had been plagued with

He had spent time
In the hospital
With excruciating pain

Said he drinks lots
Of water to insure
His piss is always clear

Since our meeting the
Guy with the taser has
Been transferred to
Another post

And I'm drinking
More water

TONY ROBLES is the co-editor and Revolutionary Worker Scholar of POOR Magazine (www.poormagazine.org), an organizing project led by indigenous and poor people that produces media by communities-in-struggle both locally and globally. He is the author of the children's books, *Lakas and the Manilatown Fish* and *Lakas and the Makibaka Hotel*. His stories are included in *Growing up Filipino II* and *Mythium Journal*. Tony was nominated for the Pushcart prize 2012. He is following in the footsteps of his uncle, the poet Al Robles.

Hibakusha

by Valerie Katagiri

In my grandmother's attic, there were boxes of clothes stored in mothballs. Among the layers of dresses, blouses, skirts, pants, and shirts, there were issues of old *Life* magazines. In one, there was a photo of a girl, white and fresh and innocent, posed Mona Lisa-like and contemplating the skull she held in one hand. The caption explained that many patriotic American soldiers sent the skulls of dead Japanese soldiers to their loved ones. The skulls had been boiled and scraped clean of their flesh. The photo was black and white ... like *Life* back then.

In my naiveté, I identified with Mona Lisa. She was the Betty Crocker in the cookbooks I pored over when learning to make pizza and hamburgers. She was the beauty who always captivated the handsome hero in the movies. She had the straight teeth and the gleaming white smile in the Crest commercials. She was the woman in the starched white nurse's uniform in the educational reels we watched in school. And there, each morning, we pledged allegiance to the flag of the United States of America that this girl lived in.

I did not understand that my non-Mona-Lisa-face confused non-Asian Americans. I have often been asked where I am from, meaning which foreign country did my ancestors come from. Saying I am American rarely satisfies White Americans: they repeat their question slowly, deliberately, but also with unmasked impatience. Sometimes their voice gets louder, as if, in addition, I must also have a hearing problem.

I think of *Life's* Mona Lisa ... did time make her wiser? Did she finally come to realize that her souvenir skull was someone who had once been alive? Someone who had probably been about her age? Who had once enjoyed a hot meal and a good night's rest?

Had once been part of a family, with a mother, a father, brothers, and sisters? Maybe had a wife and children or dreamed of one day having a family of his own? Someone who ground his teeth when things weren't going well and who laughed aloud when life was a joy? Who was afraid of dying? Who wished for a happy ending? Someone whose face had been methodically stripped naked of its distinguishing features only because he happened to be Japanese?

Grandma slowly strokes her face. She turns one way, then another, inspecting her face carefully in the mirror. She sighs. When she notices the confusion on my seven-year-old face, she forces the dimple at the corner of her mouth—that dimple that had captivated her samurai husband all those years ago. I lean my cheek against hers. She grins spontaneously. I imitate her smile, but no dimple. No Toshiro Mifune of my own, I fear. I sigh. Pout.

Grandma clucks sympathetically and proceeds to show me how she smoothes cream onto her face by stroking up and outwards. Never downwards or the skin will sag, she tells me. She lets me touch her face to prove her point. It is taut. Cool. Soft. My eyes trace her strokes. Her deformed fingers are effortless, remembering a time when they, too, were supple.

My mother admires my grandma's skin. She uses the same lotion, so they have the same comforting scent. She goes through the same ritual every morning, too. But my mother likes to tell me stories of Beppu, a little town south of Hiroshima, nestled at the northern tip of the Japanese island of Kyushu and known for its many hot springs. Mom tells me that the victims of the atomic bomb—she calls them hibakusha—had come from Hiroshima after the bombing to try to heal their radiation burns in the hot water baths in Beppu. Sadly, their journeys were often in vain.

Mom says that when she was about 8 years old, she had gone to one of those hot spring Hells and been terrified by the huge statues of leering *oni*. Their red devil faces, angry golden eyes, and twisted sneers had loomed out of white cloud-like vapors. The *oni* had brandished pitchforks in their claw-like hands as they mounted their attacks. A group of statue-children was building a tower of blocks at the feet of one of these *oni*, who then proceeded to destroy the tower so that the children had to keep re-building it over and over again.

The first time I visited Japan, my family went with my parents to Beppu so we could help my mom find her *oni*. She had been haunted by visions of her statue-children building their towers, and she thought that seeing them again would help her sleep at night. We searched all eight Hells and found her demons with angry golden eyes brandishing pitchforks for attack—but there were no statue-children building block towers that would be knocked down by ferocious devils.

Now, when we talk about searching for her oni-tortured children, she looks a little lost and bewildered.

When we were children, my brother and I would stay with my grandparents when my parents had to travel for business. What I loved most was my grandparents' *furo*. There were two huge wooden tubs in a shed next to their home. Grandpa would build a fire in the outside oven, and this would heat the water in one tub. The other tub held cold water.

We'd soap and rinse ourselves off on the concrete floor. Grandpa would fill the cold water tub with enough hot water to make a nice warm bath for us to soak in. While we soaked, Grandpa would gently soap Grandma all over. He would massage her weakened legs. Then he would lather himself and she would help him soap his back. Using a small metal ladle, he'd scoop warm water from our tub to rinse off. He and Grandma would soak at the other end of the large tub.

Sometimes, Grandpa would soak in the tub of scalding water. He would dare my brother and me to sit with him, but it was much too hot. Grandpa would chortle triumphantly, saying that one had to cultivate a strong samurai mind in order to develop a strong samurai body that could endure pain.

Some days, Grandpa would soak for awhile in a tub filled only with cold water before sitting in the hot soaking tub. He'd alternate between the two until we could hear the eventual sighs, the low murmurs in Japanese that didn't have to be translated for us to know that he was content. The hard stubborn lines on his face would relax. Even Grandma would smile, temporarily forgetting ...

... that Grandpa was having an affair. For how could a strong passionate man such as he be faithful to a woman who was half-crippled and only a shadow of the woman he'd married? She was convinced of this despite Grandpa's angry outbursts that she was a silly fool. "Baka!" he'd shout before stomping out of the house. His absences of several hours would only confirm her suspicions, and she would weep to imagine where he'd gone.

Grandma believed in dreams and she dreamt often. In a recurrent dream, she said she was riding on a bus. The bus passed the dock where men were hauling in fish and she could smell the unwashed sea on their sweating bodies. They rounded a bend and she saw a makeshift hovel among a tangle of clotheslines and laundry as she climbed out of the bus.

She went into the shack. It was dimly lit. She saw a man sewing something at an old Singer. She could hear the squeaking creak as he pumped methodically. Clackety, clackety, clackety. He didn't look up or seem to know she had come in. She moved to a dark corner near him to get a better look at what he was sewing. Still unable to make it out, she edged carefully forward so she wouldn't disturb the man's concentration.

What she saw unnerved her. The man was Grandpa and he didn't seem to be sewing anything, but he was using a lot of thread. There were mounds of fine golden thread mounted not only where a spool should have been but also where it usually wasn't. The thread gleamed in silken bunches, and she watched him pleasure his fingers through them to separate and then stroke.

Then she saw a woman come into the room to stand beside him, bending close to whisper in his ear. She sat on the stool next to him, then handed him a jar of cream. He carefully smoothed the cream into her face, upwards and outwards, stroking firmly but lovingly. The woman sighed blissfully, and her eyes glazed over.

Grandma was crying now. "Your Grandpa was touching another woman's face," she choked. "How could he?!"

Grandma cried again when she could no longer walk and had to go to a nursing home. After she had been there for about 10 years, she came to visit me in the middle of the night. She stood at the foot of my bed, not moving or saying anything, but I knew that she was trying to tell me something important. I asked her if she had found my mom's statue children. She smiled and disappeared.

When I awoke the next morning, mom called me on the phone to tell me that Grandma had died in her sleep during the night. At the time, I felt comforted that Grandma had come to say good-bye to me. Only later did I realize that Grandma had been standing, not sitting in her wheelchair as she had been forced to do at the end of her life.

On another trip to Japan with my parents, we went to the Peace Memorial Park in Hiroshima. I looked at the photos of total devastation and at the burnt victims who had suffered horribly in their last hours. I read about the acid "black rain" that ate its victims alive. I walked past wax figures whose flesh was melting off fingers and faces, hair white with ash, skin bubbling from radiation burns. I forced myself to look at the disfiguring scars and scabs that covered bodies of young women and children. There was a block of concrete with the imprint of someone who had been in the act of painting a building but was now just a shadow on the wall. I examined photos of Hiroshima before it was bombed and wondered where my great-grandparents had lived.

There were other American tourists looking at the exhibit. I heard a Caucasian mother tell her high-school-age son to look at the watch in the display. She explained how its hands had stopped at the exact time that the atomic bomb had exploded in Hiroshima, 8:15 a.m. The son said, "Cool!"

Cool? The moment when time stopped for us was "cool." This was the first time I became fully aware that although I am now an American, I am still inextricably linked to my ancestors. I am hibakusha, too.

I take some comfort and a small measure of pride that although America had knocked down much of Japan with two atomic bombs, there is now a modern Japan where shinkansen (bullet trains) whisk people back and forth at 258 mph and commerce is conducted in three-dimensional glitz and 30-feet-high video screens that flash continuously at us from tall buildings.

The distorted images of lost faces—faces with skin melting off them, caved-in holes where noses should have been, eyes that had been blinded shut—now have smooth soft skin. Like Grandma's. Like my mom's.

Still, I often am not completely sure where I belong. I am without a country. I am an American, but to the majority among whom I live, my face isn't. I look like those in Japan, but to the majority who live there, I am not Japanese.

It's been awhile since my grandma's visit to me. I am talking to my mother on the phone again. Mom says she's had the strangest dream. Mom believes in her dreams, too. In her dream, Grandma came to tell her there were two *nasubi* ready to be picked in her garden. Grandma loved her eggplant cooked in shoyu and Mom often would cook the *nasubi* to her liking and bring some to her. In the dream, Mom asks Grandma if she wants her *nasubi* cooked with sardines. Grandma says no, just season hers. So, in her dream, my mom cooks the nasubi and only adds the sardines to her portion.

Mom tells me that she doesn't always remember her dreams, but because she remembered this one, she went to her garden to check her *nasubi* plants (which she hadn't done recently). There were two huge *nasubi* hanging from the plant and their weight made them nearly touch the earth. Had Mom waited another day, they probably would have settled to the ground and begun to rot. Mom says she picked them ... cooked them ... and, eating Grandma's favorite food, thought about her again.

VALERIE KATAGIRI is an award-winning author of several *Writer's Digest* entries, including "Love Tales" and "Nine Lives." She was a finalist in *Glimmer Train's* short story contest and was also a Special Award cash prize winner in the "A Brief Message from the Heart" letter-writing contest. She has been a monthly contributor to a senior newspaper in Portland, Oregon and is currently ghost-writing a parenting book as well as working on a book of her own. She is very pleased to be a co-editor for this Asian American anthology project because of her love for Asians, Americans, and anthologies.

Across the Ocean

by Michael Lai

Forty-five years ago, I was a schoolboy in Taiwan. I moved to the United States when I was 17 and haven't returned to Taiwan since that long ago time ... except in my memories. Like a lot of Chinese, my background is complicated. I was born in Burma of a Hunanese father and Fujianese mother. My father spoke with a heavy Hunanese accent, while my mother spoke in the standard Mandarin that she had picked up in school even though her mother tongue was Fujianese. We kids never learned to speak Hunanese; it was a difficult dialect, and not many people spoke it in Taiwan. I started talking around the time that my father was stationed at the Chinese (Republic of China, not the communist China) Embassy in Iran. There I learned a smidgeon of Farsi but mainly attended an American school, so early on in life, English became my mother tongue.

My family returned to Taiwan around 1959. It was quite a shock. American schools treat students with kid gloves. You developed on your own, according to your natural abilities and creativity. In Taiwan, students led a regimented life. You had to wear khaki uniforms and tennis shoes. Colorful street clothes and leather shoes were forbidden. Students marched to the flag-raising ceremony each morning before class.

We had to sweep the classroom floors and dust the tables. Each morning, before class, we had a health inspection. Students were expected to bring a facemask, a few sheets of toilet paper (they didn't come in rolls), gauze, and a drinking cup. At inspection time, each row selected a row monitor who would go up and down the row, inspecting your nails for dirt; you flipped your palms up and down so the monitor could check for cleanliness. Most unusual of all, they looked behind your ears to make sure they were not dirty. Students brought their lunches in metal boxes called *bien dan*, and everyone put their *bien dan* in a large wicker basket, whereupon the school workers hauled them to be steamed in time for lunch. Thus you got a hot meal even though the school didn't provide school lunches.

The minute the teacher walked in, the class president would announce, "*Chi Li*," meaning stand up. After we bowed to the teacher and resumed our seats, the teacher would start teaching.

Discipline was rigid in Taiwanese schools. If you didn't do your homework, the teacher would use a rattan cane and whip your palm. Sometimes the palm got hit so hard it would swell up. I dreaded going to school because I had been raised in an American missionary school where corporal punishment was unheard of. Taiwan needed a lot of getting used to.

Taiwan was on a war footing with the communists on the mainland. The whole country was geared toward building up the country, counterattacking and recovering the mainland, and all the students from early grade school to the end of high school were inculcated with the great mission of taking back the mainland and rescuing our brethren there, where they lived in pits of "deep water and hot fires." Almost every student's essays would end with the exhortation "We must do well because we have to recover the mainland and rescue our brethren." The whole country was subjected to this propaganda. It was a bit unnerving to be so regimented, but the upside was that students rarely had behavioral and drug problems or got involved in criminal activities. American schoolchildren, on the other hand, enjoy many rights, including the right to wear anything they want, citing freedom of expression. Teachers don't dare discipline American schoolchildren for fear their parents will raise a ruckus. Consequently, American teachers spend an inordinate amount of time maintaining discipline in class, and the students get short-changed in instruction time. Their learning suffers.

The Taiwanese countryside was beautiful. In the spring, the paddies were full of water and the farmers bent over to plant rice seedlings in the mud. They wore conical hats made from bamboo leaves. It kept the sun out and often shielded the head from rain.

After a hard day's work, the farmer's kid would lead the water buffalo down to a deep part of an irrigation ditch and let the animal cool off in the water. It was quite a sight to walk over a footbridge and see a pair of horns sticking out of the water, and upon closer scrutiny, a pair of huge nostrils that blew water vapor with a grunt. In the fields where the buffaloes chewed their cud, you would invariably see a blackbird perched upon their backs. It was a symbiotic relationship. The bird ate insects and other bugs that bothered the buffalo, and the buffalo gently accommodated the bird, never chasing it away.

Walking the streets of my rural hometown, Yung Ho Dseng, actually a suburb of Taipei across the Tamshui River, my ears were accosted by the noisy clatter of wood clogs. They were called *tuo ban*, literally meaning "drag block of wood." Back then, Taiwanese were too poor to afford leather shoes or sandals, and the plastic industry was barely flowering. Almost everybody wore *tuo ban*, a piece of wood fashioned into the shape of a sandal or clog, with a strap of plastic in front to hold the sandal securely to the foot. People dragged the sandal while they walked and it created quite a noise, a clitter clacker that is hard to describe: basically the sound of a wooden pallet striking the hard surface of concrete. I wonder how the Dutch countryside sounded when the Dutch used to wear their wooden cobble shoes, shaped like a boat.

Sometimes I would accompany my mother to the open farmer's market. There were no supermarkets then, and markets were held in parts of town away from vehicle traffic. Mostly pedestrians and pedicabs. These markets were dirty and wet, with puddles of water and potholes everywhere. But the food was fresh. Chinese preferred fresh food from the fields, still muddy and wet from a cursory rinsing in dirty ditch water. Fish and meat were laid out in the open, no refrigeration and no ice. It was easy to tell which fish were fresh and which had been on the crates for some time.

Housewives and servants shopped with wicker or bamboo baskets. The merchants didn't provide grocery bags or plastic bags. The most you got was a fish or piece of meat wrapped in newspaper. Vegetables were shoved into the shoppers' baskets with leaves and stems sticking out, sort of like the American

Thanksgiving cornucopia. If we go back to shopping green for the environment, we would be going back at least 45 years to that era when I was a little kid, with mother carrying a wicker basket, no plastic bags, no wrappings, expect for some old newspapers wet from wrapping a fish or piece of pork.

Taiwanese ate pork because beef was a costly luxury. Taiwanese farmers also did not like butchering their prized buffalo, because they could not bring themselves to eat an animal that had faithfully toiled and tilled for them. There was no beef industry, and most of the beef came from slaughtered water buffaloes. Some restaurants would advertise that their beef was from *huang niu*, meaning "yellow cows," most probably an imported livestock not native to Taiwan, and therefore expensive and only for the well-to-do or businessmen who entertained their clients with a bowl of hot beef stew noodles (the famous Taiwanese *la nio rou mien*).

Transportation was mainly by bus, pedicabs or the two legs, nicknamed The Eleventh bus route because the number 11 resembled two legs. Taking the bus was an adventure in "sardine packing" or *ji sha ding yu*. When the bus came to a stop, nobody queued. Everybody scrambled for the bus entrance and elbowed or fought their way in. I was small and short, and if I didn't get a seat I would stand packed among the passengers unable to reach the overhead straps. So I swayed and moved along with the rhythms of the bus. The most agonizing moments came when the bus came to a hard stop, and everybody would sway in one direction, then another, like a wave. It was easy to feel smothered. Luckily I wasn't susceptible to motion sickness.

I remember one year, new buses came into service. They were yellow and had a flat front instead of an elongated engine front. These yellow buses had the engine compartment inside, right next to the driver. To the right of the driver, next to the engine cover, were two up-front seats highly coveted by school children who fought to sit in one of them. Back then, it didn't take much to impress or delight schoolchildren. Those flat-fronted buses, called *bien tou che*, really caused some excitement for a while. I wonder what the buses in Taiwan look like now.

I confess that I am now a spoiled American and have not ridden a bus in years, except for those short rides at airport terminals. I haven't had to be squeezed like a sardine in a can for decades. I hope I, and others like me, have progressed. Yet a nagging feeling keeps haunting me. If we don't jam pack into buses, that means we each drive a half ton of metal to work and back every day, burning up fossil fuels and polluting the air. So have we progressed or regressed? I don't know. Sometimes the old ways may be better.

I was 17 when I came to the U.S. to join my brother who was in college. He had arranged for a local high school to accept me as an exchange student. Immigration rules were lax then, so I had no problem getting an I-20, a permit to study in a U.S. school.

I landed at Sea-Tac airport in Seattle. My brother had to go back to school, so he arranged for an American friend to meet me. I grew up in Taiwan thinking of the U.S. as being Washington D.C., New York City, and Chicago. And here I was, in the Pacific Northwest, going to Pullman, WA. A place I'd never heard of. And no wonder. Pullman was a little college town stuck in the middle of nowhere in Washington state's wheat country, called Palouse country or the Inland Empire. The news at 6 o'clock was local, and talked about places I'd never heard of, like Klitickat or Snoqualmie Pass or—weirdest of all—Spokane, which Washingtonians pronounce Spo-Kan, not Spo-Cain. If the TV color wasn't adjusted correctly, the announcers' faces became a garish pink or the background a weird purple. Welcome to the world of color television.

Come time for me to travel to Pullman by Greyhound bus, I found myself eating lunch at the Greyhound bus cafeteria. Suddenly I got a nosebleed, but nobody would help me until a Filipino busboy saw my plight and handed over a wad of napkins. It was then that I realized that Asians are pretty much invisible in the U.S., and Asians actually were more inclined to look out for each other. Back then, 45 years ago, Asians were an oddity in Washington state and I'm sure in most of the U.S.

The trip to Pullman was eye-opening. I saw the mighty Cascade Mountain range, evergreen forests and tall mountain peaks.

As we moved into wheat country, I was struck by all the wide-open spaces. Acres and acres of wheat fields and nothingness, and wonder of wonders, I did not see hundreds of farmers bent over, hoeing and planting. It seemed like in this part of the U.S., food grew naturally without any human intervention. Of course, that was not true. It was because everything was mechanized. One farmer could drive a tractor and plow hundreds of acres; machinery harvested crops, so you never saw hordes of farmers in the fields doing backbreaking work.

One year, one of my American roommates invited me to his home for the holidays. His dad was an apple farmer, located smack dab in Wenatchee County, the apple capital of America. One day, they took me to the nearest big town, Wenatchee, to shop around. I came across a store that carried, of all things, cans of fish balls (*yu wan*).

I was both intrigued and surprised that I would find such a food in an obscure corner of the state, where Asians were a minority of minorities. I bought a can and invited them to try it out over dinner. They just chuckled and declined, thinking it was some strange food. "Fish balls in soup?" asked my roommate, half teasing. "You don't mean fish testicles, do you?" I didn't know enough to tell him that it was merely fish meat ground into a paste, mixed with starch to make a fish-flavored meatball. Back then, Americans had never heard of sashimi and sushi. They were mainly meat and potatoes people and looked at most Oriental cuisine as strange and something to laugh at and chuckle over.

Times have changed. Now I live in Northern California, where Mongolian barbecues and sushi places are all over the city, and actually, a lot of Caucasians enjoy that stuff probably more than me.

Back in college, I went to a small grocery store operated by the only Asian family in Pullman. The owner lady looked at me as an oddity. She remarked that the students from Taiwan were so careful with their money. One Taiwanese girl took a long time to decide to buy even a couple of eggs even when the supermarket price was 17 cents a dozen. Taiwan and China were poor countries in those days. Families had to scrimp and save and borrow to send students abroad to study.

I used to walk over 2 miles in the evening so I could use the one free telephone at the school library. And calls were only 10 cents back then. There used to be a commercial that said "I'd walk a mile for a Camel." For me and other Taiwanese students, it was "I'd walk a mile to save a dime." To put things in perspective, gas was about 37 cents a gallon, and often, gas stations across the street would engage in price wars, lowering their prices to attract customers. They often gave out free maps and coffee mugs. Those days are gone now. I miss the full service gas stations, where the minute you pulled in, attendants would gas you up, check the oil under the hood, and if requested, check the air in your tires. They'd also wash your windshields for you. Dinosaurs aren't the only things that have disappeared from the face of the earth.

Then in the 1970s, I started to hear about rich Taiwanese businessmen plunking down cash to buy San Francisco houses. No mortgage needed, just pay cash in one lump sum. When I heard this rumor, I couldn't believe it. I remember my student days when I was dirt poor and worked every holiday I could to earn tuition money, as did most of my fellow Taiwanese and Hong Kong students. And now my countrymen were paying cash for Bay Area houses. It was an incredible change, as much of a change as sushi buffets, ramen restaurants, Mongolian barbecues and Thai noodle places. And of course, we can't ignore the Vietnamese who have transformed entire sections of cities into Little Saigons with their markets, restaurants and various businesses. Asians have become the majority in California communities such as Alhambra, Monterey Park, and San Gabriel. We hear about Korea Towns and Little Saigons. In my youth, Asians were a minority, to be stared at like aliens from outer space.

Now, we have become doctors, engineers, lawyers, pharmacists, and to my satisfaction, clerks at DMVs, Walmart stores, mechanics, and even gardeners. We have become more mainstream, not just stereotypical eggheads. Who would have thought that 17-year-old boy from Taiwan would be witness to so many changes ... be nostalgic for his early years in Taiwan ... but also grateful to have lived through two quite different lives in his 62 years.

MICHAEL LAI emigrated from Taiwan to the U.S. in 1968 and finished high school in Pullman, WA. He then attended Washington State University, graduating with a degree in psychology. After WSU, he attended Oregon State University in Corvallis, Oregon, where he received his pharmacy degree. He retired from full-time pharmacy work in 2008 and now spends his time puttering around, planning travels with his wife, doing some relief pharmacy work, and writing. His three adult children live in different parts of the world, and he looks forward to visits with them.

My Brother—The Keeper

by Dmae Roberts

I just saw my little brother, Jack, digging through a Dumpster at our neighborhood grocery store, and I pretended I didn't know him. He was in the dirty, torn clothes he likes to wear for what he calls "collecting." Sometimes his flannel shirts and fleece jackets are hanging in shreds on his thin, middle-aged frame. I know he doesn't eat well, even though I buy him food, and every time I see him, he looks thinner. Though he can afford a haircut, he lets his hair grow long and stringy; when he perspires, it clings to his face and the old, thick glasses he wears.

When I moved him from our mother's home in Eugene, where he'd lived until her death three years ago, to a nice one-bedroom house around the corner from me in Portland, I naively thought that in new surroundings his behavior would change. I've begged, cajoled, and criticized. But he won't stop. Jack doesn't dig through Dumpsters for income: collecting is his joy, his passion in life, one I'll never understand.

Back at home, sitting at my cluttered desk, I fight the urge to phone him and ask again why he won't stop. I've done my research, read about disposophobia—the fear of getting rid of junk. I've rationalized that Jack isn't as bad as the people you see on the news who hoard dozens of small animals in their homes; he's just a pack rat with a strong compulsion. A year ago, I took him to counseling, but after eight weeks of sessions, the mental health expert concluded, much to my frustration, that Jack was too old to change his behavior and that I needed to stop getting upset about it. That made me angry—but I knew Jack wasn't the only one in the family with a problem.

When I got married ten years ago and my husband moved into my small bungalow, we labored over how to fit his stuff into my two-bedroom house—one of the bedrooms was my dedicated office. For a while, the dining room became my husband's office and dressing room, but then the house got so crammed that he built a two-story garage; my office was on top. It was heaven to have all that space. Four years later, the garage is stacked full of home-remodeling supplies and boxes I cleared out of the basement. In my office I have three desks, each one piled with paper because I hate filing. Business cards and small writing pads are stashed behind my computer monitor because I haven't figured out what to do with them. Every time I begin to clean up, an urge to travel suddenly overtakes me: I long for a nice clean hotel room without piles of stuff lying around. The only problem is that I always come back home to face the clutter again.

As a child, I lived with my family on a two-acre farm in the small town of Junction City, Oregon. My family had so little. What we did have, we hung onto till it broke. My dad piled old washers, dryers, refrigerators, and a broken kitchen sink outside the house. He said it cost too much to haul junk away, and it was good to have spare parts in case he needed to fix something. My mom bought everything on sale, so there were boxes and bags of bulk items, and we ate food years past its expiration date. My brother and I got one pair of shoes at the beginning of the school year, and we got new ones only when those completely wore out and even duct tape wouldn't protect our feet.

Both of my parents were survivors: my mom grew up in the ravaged countryside of Taiwan during World War II, and my dad was a child of Depression-era parents in dust bowl Oklahoma. They had experienced poverty on two different sides of the world. Both of them knew the value of a dollar and the meaning of living without. Although they valued different things, they both hoarded.

When I took a break from college and traveled to Taiwan, my parents divorced after decades of fighting over money and cultural differences. My mom wanted more possessions and an income that would allay her constant fear of being poor and starving again as she had in her childhood. My dad just wanted to chew the fat with neighbors and fix things on the farm.

After the divorce, my dad got a one-bedroom apartment of his own, and my mother got the house and most of the possessions. My dad thought he'd get a fresh start, but he died from heart failure a couple of years later. I cleaned out his apartment after the funeral and got rid of his secondhand furniture and appliances. In his wallet he'd kept childhood photos of my brother and me and an IOU for $200 from a friend. His nightstand had dozens of cigarette burns next to the ashtray, and the drawer was full of methamphetamine samples he got from his doctor to help him lose weight. I sifted through odd clues about this man I didn't really know as well as I'd thought. The week before he died, we'd argued because he wanted money for the car he'd given me. When I was cleaning out his apartment that had so little in it, I realized he'd asked me for money only because he really needed it. I regretted our last fight for a long time.

My mom died two decades later, after a three-year battle with breast cancer. Cleaning out her house was a monumental task because she'd saved everything. Her lifelong dream was to open a Chinese restaurant; she had enough boxes full of plates, bowls, and tea kettles to stock several restaurants. Mom had three closets full of clothes, most of which were finds from Goodwill or sequined dresses she'd brought back from Taiwan, "cheap." She had one dresser for underwear and another dresser for shirts and pants mingled with silver coin collections and envelopes stuffed with family photos from several decades. Her bathroom drawers held new and used makeup, Oil of Olay bottles, Chanel No. 5 perfumes, bars of soap, and bottles of shampoo and conditioner piled in corners. One container in the living room was dedicated to grocery coupons clipped years ago. Her Buddhist altar room had a closet stacked with incense for her temple. The garage was stuffed with bits of broken furniture she called "antiques," an old piano that didn't play, and a freezer full of frozen food dating back several years. The sheer bulk of the items she'd hoarded could have fed, clothed, and furnished several families.

Hoarding isn't unusual for war survivors or for children of the Depression era, who feel the compulsion to store up just in case of another impending catastrophe. But my brother and I inherited the same desire to hang onto things, "just in case." For me, it's a connection to memories I find hard to let go of. For my brother, collecting is more of an escape.

He had a rough time growing up among bullies who picked on him all through elementary and high school—though we were both from the only interracial family in town, he looked more Chinese than I. Some days, kids yelled racial slurs at him and threw his schoolbooks into the toilet in the boys' bathroom. Other days they simply roughed him up. My dad talked to the high school principal, who said they couldn't do anything about it, that my brother just needed to tough it out. Instead, my brother retreated to a private world on the farm. When he came home from school, he enjoyed trudging through mud in knee-high rubber boots to herd the chickens and cows that had broken out of the fence. To save money and keep the farm animals fed, my mom enlisted my brother to forage through Dumpsters at our local grocery stores and the pizza parlor. I was deeply ashamed that my family dug through trash. I retreated into school, choir, and drama activities, doing my best to disassociate myself from my family. But my brother continued the back-alley pursuit of getting free stuff even after he graduated from high school.

After my dad died, my brother was left to care for my mom, who was quite dependent because she didn't read or write and wasn't a safe driver. When they left the farm and moved to Eugene, he continued his passion for Dumpster diving by collecting bottles. I first discovered the depths of his compulsion when I went to stay with them to help care for her while she was being treated for cancer. He had filled an entire room in the house and half of the garage with grocery bags of bottles. Beer bottles were separated from pop bottles. Most had been washed and their labels removed. Some bags were full of broken glass. He told me he turned in the good bottles for the deposit, but with each visit, I saw the bags were still there. When I asked him why he hadn't returned them, he replied that he had and that those bottles were new ones.

More bottles would appear, washed and sorted by size and shape. When my mom died and he and I went through the house to get rid of her things, the bottles remained. When I moved him to Portland to be closer to me, his bottles came with him. I didn't know this until I saw the bags in the tool shed of his new house. I'd thought he could make a fresh start, but when I questioned him, he shyly shut down, his fists clenched and his face red. He couldn't explain why he needed his bottles.

His hoarding compulsion frightened me because I'd felt the urge myself. I'd watched my parents litter our home with stuff and had vowed I would never need possessions to make me happy. I carefully monitored my brother to keep him from being engulfed by the dark morass of his collections. I was scared for him, but I was scared for myself, too.

In the days before a friend comes to visit, I'm a cyclone of energy, throwing piles of stuff into recycling bags and hiding things under the bed, in drawers, in filing cabinets and already full closets. As I get older, I hang onto souvenirs for emotional reasons. I have boxes of old reel-to-reel recordings from my early days in radio, bins filled with daily journals, photo albums I need to digitize, record albums with covers I love, a wooden clarinet I quit playing in high school, the guitar I bought in Hong Kong and took to Dublin to sing "The Night They Drove Old Dixie Down." The long shiny scarves I've bought on every trip abroad since the eighties are tucked into the black hole that is my closet.

I hate holding onto things and envy friends who do spring cleaning anytime of the year. Every time I get a notice from the Vietnam Vets or the ARC to donate unused items, I force myself to fill the donation bags. I reflect on the memories associated with each object I give away and try to let go of them before they envelop and swallow me. Perhaps I understand too well why my brother holds onto empty bottles: it's the same way I hold onto mementos of my life.

DMAE ROBERTS, a two-time Peabody-winning writer/producer, has created groundbreaking personal, multicultural documentaries. Her Peabody Award-winning documentary, *Mei Mei, a Daughter's Song*, is a harrowing account of her mother's childhood in Taiwan during WWII. The eight-hour Peabody-winning *Crossing East* is the first Asian American history series on public radio. She is a United States Artist fellow and is working on her memoir, *Lady Buddha and the Temple of Ma*. Her stage play, *Picasso In The Back Seat*, won the Oregon Book Award. Her essays have been published in the *Oregon Humanities Journal* ("My Brother—The Keeper"), *Temple University Press* ("But Still, Like Air I'll Rise"), and *The Sun Magazine* ("Cooking in a Storm"). Her essay "Finding The Poetry" was published in *Radio Reality* (UNC Press). She is currently associate producer of *Shakespeare Is* and writes a column for Portland's *Asian Reporter*.

Double Suicide:
The Deaths of Ernest Hemingway
and Iris Chang Reconsidered

by Darrell Y. Hamamoto

Five decades after his suicide by shotgun, it appears that what had been assumed to be simple paranoia on the part of literary giant Ernest Hemingway was in fact grounded in the reality of his systematic persecution by certain elements within the US government. Veteran writer A. E. Hotchner, a close friend and author of the classic biography *Papa Hemingway* (1966), recounted the days spent with a demoralized, confused, and frustrated individual who was struggling to complete basic creative tasks central to his work. Hemingway had contacted Hotchner in May 1960 to ask for his help in editing an overly-long article that had been commissioned by *Life* magazine. In an article published July 01, 2011 (*New York Times*), Hotchner now realizes that government harassment and surveillance by wiretaps, tax audits, and pharmacologically-induced mind control claimed by his increasingly harried and depressed friend were indeed valid.[1]

The revelation that Hemingway had been targeted for surveillance by the government intelligence unit headed by J. Edgar Hoover is consistent with a well-documented history of American citizens held under suspicion by the FBI or the scores of other less well-known spy agencies within the government, military, and civilian sectors.[2] There is a bounty of literature that raises disturbing questions about the murder of individuals ranging from community organizers such as Fred Hampton to prominent artists such as John Lennon.[3] The examples of assassination as politics by other means abound: JFK, Malcolm

X, Martin Luther King, Robert F. Kennedy. According to opinion polls, the overwhelming majority of Americans today do not believe the official findings of the Warren Commission that had been formed to investigate the public killing of President John F. Kennedy in November 1963.[4]

It is in this historical context that the seemingly paranoid claims made by Iris Chang in the months prior to her death in 2004 must be taken seriously. Chang had become a literary sensation at age twenty-nine with the publication of the incendiary study *The Rape of Nanking* (1997).[5] Like Hemingway, Chang also died by her own hand. On November 9, 2004, she was found dead in her car that was parked on an isolated road near Los Gatos, California. It was determined that Chang had taken her own life with a pistol she had purchased the day before the incident. She was thirty-six years old.

Former journalism school classmate and personal friend Paula Kamen advanced the notion that the Chang suicide was the result of "mental illness." She first had believed the "dark topics" that Chang was writing about had drove her over the edge, but then concluded that the ambitious author suffered from "bipolar disorder."[6] In *Finding Iris Chang* (2008), Kamen interprets her friend's demise through the lens of the medico-pharmacological orthodoxy that has come to predominate throughout a society that is viewed as being composed of sick and debilitated individuals that suffer from an ever-lengthening list of ailments grouped under the heading of "mental illness."[7] The "mental illness" characterization was rejected out of hand by Ying-Ying Chang in *The Woman Who Could Not Forget* (2011). As her mother, it was she who had been the principal person caring for Iris Chang during her final months of dark despair. Instead, she points to the side effects caused by experimental "anti-psychotic" drugs prescribed by a succession of psychiatrists as responsible for the downward spiral of a spirited woman who, although sensitive, never before betrayed signs of so-called mental illness.[8]

Kamen herself suffered from chronic pain and the overriding theme of her book on Chang is that the revolution in anti-depressant pharmacology has been a boon to the sad and afflicted masses. Against Kamen, however, there is a sizeable and growing body of literature that traces the less-than-altruistic origins of psychopharmacology in the mind control human experiments conducted by the CIA beginning in the 1950s. Based upon documents that saw limited release due to pressure from the US Congress and its Church Committee investigation, *The Search for the "Manchurian Candidate"* (1979) by John Marks is a good place to start for those ignorant of government initiatives in mind management and political pacification.[9] More recent publications issued from perfectly respectable quarters (as opposed to those tagged as "conspiracy" buffs) contend that the system of mind control research, development, and application remains in place albeit in a far more sophisticated guise.[10]

The pervasiveness of pharmacological mind control is evident to anyone (i.e. anyone not on psychotropic medication) who works in a classroom environment with the current generation of students who have been labeled as "depressed" or plagued by "attention deficit disorder" and are then promiscuously prescribed selective serotonin reuptake inhibitors (SSRIs).[11] Young people who would otherwise be in prime physical and intellectual condition have been transformed into zombie-like creatures whose flat affect and deadened eyes betray their forced chemical romance with the military-pharmacological complex.[12]

According to Hotchner, Hemingway complained that the Feds had his telephones tapped and his automobile and rooms bugged. His mail was being intercepted and sifted through. He was being tailed as well. Then Hemingway was admitted to St. Mary's Hospital in Rochester, Minnesota in November 1960 for psychiatric treatment. He underwent electro-shock therapy and endured eleven separate sessions. Hemingway became even more depressed and attempted suicide on more than one occasion. In response to Hotchner asking him why he wanted to kill himself, Hemingway said that everything he valued in life—friends, sex, health, and creative work—had been taken from him. He ended his life on July 02, 1961. Documents acquired through the Freedom of Information Act indicate that Hemingway had been under FBI surveillance since the 1940s.

Prior to her suicide, Chang had told those close to her that "powerful" forces linked to the government were closing in on her. She left written statements that unambiguously outlined the contours of the plot laid against her while attempting to complete an historical account of the "Bataan Death March" as it is known popularly. Most attributed her mounting "paranoia" to stress, overwork, and exposure to stories told to her by survivors. Chang was also a new mother, so some felt that this only compounded matters. Although Chang hid the fact, Kamen discovered that her son had been adopted. This ruled out the "post-partum depression" theory.

In one of the notes addressed to her parents, Chang wrote:

> There are aspects of my experience in Louisville [in a mental hospital in August 2004] that I will never understand. Deep down I suspect that you may have more answers about this than I do. I can never shake my belief that I was being recruited, and later persecuted, by forces more powerful than I could have imagined. Whether it was the CIA or some other organization, I will never know. As long as I'm alive, these forces will never stop hounding me ... .
>
> Days before I left for Louisville, I had a deep foreboding about my safety. I sensed suddenly threats to my own life: an eerie feeling that I was being followed in the streets, the white van parked outside my house, damaged mail arriving at my P.O. Box. I believe my detention at Norton Hospital was the government's attempt to discredit me.
>
> I had considered running away, but I will never be able to escape from myself and my thoughts. I am doing this because I am too weak to withstand the years of pain and agony ahead.[13]

Read in proper context, these words make perfect sense. They are far from being the ravings of a "paranoiac." Ying-Ying Chang, who suspects that Japanese rightists might have been responsible for the harassment of her daughter, accepts the claims of Iris Chang that she had been approached personally and threatened.

Nor does she dismiss the possibility that images of "horrible atrocities and ugly images of children torn apart by wars" had been streamed purposely to the television set of the Louisville hotel where Chang had been staying while on a research trip.

In acting as unofficial spokesperson for the post-1965 Taiwanese American cohort composed of scientists and engineers who were pushing for a stronger political voice commensurate with their significantly large representation within the academic/military/corporate complex, Chang had the temerity to accuse the US government and President George W. Bush of attempting to stonewall the movement by Taiwanese Americans pressing its demands for reparations to those who suffered at the hands of the Imperial government during World War II. Since Japan is an important US ally in East Asia it was thought that Washington was loath to support an initiative that would harm the postwar relationship and consensus formed between the top two economic powerhouses in the world.

Predictably, assertions that ultranationalist Japanese elements in some way were implicated in the death of Chang appeared online and in print almost immediately after the news of her suicide appeared. She became a martyr for the truth in the People's Republic of China but especially among overseas Chinese in the US. In the former case, reminders of the "Asian Holocaust" perpetrated by Imperial Japan has been a useful tool in the hands of the Communist oligarchs to deflect attention from the tens of millions of fellow Chinese that were sacrificed to consolidate power during the reign of Mao.[14] Today, orchestrated anti-Japan agitation via the internet helps maintain one-party dictatorial control in a nation roiling with internal conflict and rebellion in its far flung regions.

For Taiwanese Americans—a large number (including both parents of Chang who earned Ph.D.s at Harvard) of whom have been recruited since the 1950s specifically to staff highly specialized positions within (ironically) the death-dealing US military-industrial complex—the "Asian Holocaust" has been an effective rallying point in attaining the level of political clout that matches their professional status and economic standing.[15]

Moreover, a shared historical memory of the widespread destruction and atrocities committed by the Imperial Japanese military during World War II eases political tensions between the PRC and Taiwan via a shared sense of victimhood directed against Japan. At the same time, the US arms industry continues to reap enormous profits through the sale of aircraft, communications systems, and all manner of advanced weaponry to Taiwan despite protests by PRC officials. Complicating the campaign to promote memory of the "Asian Holocaust," a number of highly placed Chinese Americans have been implicated in brokering the transfer of strategically sensitive American satellite and missile technology to the People's Liberation Army.[16]

In the battle over historical memory and the role that Iris Chang played in massaging it, however, there is one possible scenario that has been overlooked: that she might have been silenced for having ventured too close to truths that if exposed would have put the US—not Japan—in a most unflattering light. More significantly, the investigative trail she was following with her most recent book project involving The Philippines could have led to wider exposure of the not widely known historical circumstances that undergird the very basis of the postwar economic and political order led by the US.

An incredible book that went largely un-reviewed by the corporate press was published by the independent Verso imprint in 2003 titled *Gold Warriors: America's Secret Recovery of Yamashita's Gold*, written by Sterling and Peggy Seagrave.[17] Well-researched and thoroughly documented (including a CD containing facsimiles of original papers), the book reveals the process whereby hundreds of tons of precious metals, gems, and countless art treasures that had been looted by the Japanese Imperial Army throughout Asia fell into the hands of Ferdinand Marcos and his cronies in the waning days of World War II en route to Japan where they would be kept as spoils of war. The vast quantity of gold bullion produced from the booty that came into the possession of the United States was instrumental in the postwar economic recovery of Japan. America's special friend Marcos had succeeded in locating much of "Yamashita's gold" thanks to the torture of key informants who pointed to vast stores of purloined wealth that had been cleverly hidden.

Iris Chang began her career as a hard-charging and ambitious crusader for truth. Beginning with her first book, *Thread of the Silkworm* (1996), she only touched upon the duplicity of government and the utter cynicism in which its interests are pursued.[18] The subject of the work, research scientist Tsien Hsue-Shen who helped found the Jet Propulsion Laboratory at Caltech, was sacrificed to anti-Red hysteria that took hold when the Communist Party came to power with the Chinese Revolution. With *The Rape of Nanking*, Chang discovered that historical truth is never self-evident nor is it necessarily welcomed. This is the point at which she might possibly have come to the realization that *real politik* was grounded in cynicism, opportunism, and exploitation. The political-economic oligarchs that use government for their own purposes will tolerate and even encourage truth-seeking up to a point. After all, these elite families dole out millions of dollars each year in sophisticated tax-avoidance and wealth-maintenance schemes to all manner of idealists, reformers, and truth-tellers through private foundations bearing their names. Should anyone come too close to exposing the source of their totalistic power, however, like the Venetian families of old they will not hesitate to have such persons eliminated. Poisons have been their proven specialty.

So long as the work of Iris Chang satisfied the agendas of the different interest groups, governmental entities, and political factions that benefitted from the good will and public sympathy garnered by *The Rape of Nanking*, she functioned as a useful asset. But with her final book project, thorough and meticulous researcher that she was, Chang independently of the Seagraves might have uncovered truths that would undermine the very foundation of the US monetary system, which had been taken off the gold standard by President Richard Nixon in 1971. Not coincidentally, early in his political career, Nixon reportedly received large cash payments from Ferdinand Marcos who, as dictator of The Philippines, enjoyed political and generous financial support from the US.[19] Ed Rollins, former campaign director for Ronald Reagan, wrote of ten million US dollars allegedly handed over by high-level political operators from the Philippines.[20] Indeed, structural corruption has defined the relationship between the US and the Philippines from colonial times to present.[21] Quite possibly, Chang had found during the course of her research and political involvement on behalf of those who experienced profound losses during wartime, that her own American government was complicit if not at the center of the multiple holocausts of the twentieth century.

In August 2004, while conducting interviews with survivors of Bataan in Louisville, Kentucky, Chang exhibited signs of mental instability. With the assistance of a certain "Colonel Kelly" whose presence she stated had frightened her severely, Chang was committed to the Norton Psychiatric Hospital. There, she was diagnosed as having experienced a "brief reactive psychosis."

For at least three days, Chang was subjected to "antipsychotic" drugs until her parents arrived to take their daughter back to California. Once returned home, she was placed on a regimen of "anti-depressants" that did little to improve her condition. Brett Douglas, the IT professional to whom she was married, appeared to offer scant emotional support to his wife other than insisting that she hew to the treatment prescribed her by medical professionals. His seeming callousness toward her was remarked upon by Kamen in *Finding Iris Chang* when upon visiting with Douglas at his home for an interview, she was introduced to a Chinese woman also named "Iris." He had met her online only months after the suicide death of his wife.

In an age when Big Pharma has succeeded in enslaving an alarmingly large percentage of American women to SSRIs— commonly known as "anti-depressants"—the death of Iris Chang should serve as a cautionary warning. The historical origins of the psychiatric dictatorship lie in the Cold War mind control experiments known collectively as MK-ULTRA.[22] Instead, the totalitarian triumph of the medico-pharmacological model combined with the so-called "mental health" establishment is embraced and welcomed by well-intentioned but dangerously compromised medical professionals and psychotherapists held in the thrall of the insurance industry and drug makers.

Although the "suicides" of Ernest Hemingway and Iris Chang are separated in time by close to five decades, they are connected in a closed loop formed by the dark history of authoritarian regimes that actively suppress the truths that would subvert their rule. The oligarchs will go so far as to order that the life force be snuffed out of those who dare bring light to the world. Instead of murdering directly two well-admired literary figures of worldwide stature and thereby run the risk of official inquiries, Hemingway and Chang were harassed, gang-stalked, and psychiatrically maimed to the point where they found it too painful to live.

The twin orthodoxy of psychiatry and pharmacy provided the respectable cover to preclude a closer look into the deaths of Hemingway and Chang. As it was in the case of Hemingway, however, the death of Iris Chang is not a closed book. Further investigation into the circumstances of her mental breakdown, coerced psychiatric treatment, and the identification of persons such as the mysterious "Colonel Kelly" who had her committed in Louisville, will shatter the easy and conveniently premature conclusion that the death of Chang was due to so-called "mental illness" alone.

In time, it will be seen that in her death, the final gift to humankind bequeathed by Iris Chang will be the exposure of the system announced in 1969 by José M. R. Delgado of Yale University in *Physical Control of the Mind*.[23] Chang was far from being "mad" or "paranoid." Rather, Chang to the very end was engaged in a quite sane but desperate struggle for the recovery of the humanity that had been stripped from her. Instead of allowing herself to be forced into a permanent state of narcotized semi-awareness and zombie-like passivity, Chang mustered the courage to end her life by a method so disturbing and sensational that questions concerning the circumstances leading to this final act of resistance will be asked far into the future. This is made clear in the intimate account given by Ying-Ying Chang who was closely involved with her daughter in seeking therapeutic approaches that, in the end, failed to restore the *élan vital* that had been sapped by fear and loathing.

In this, Chang left the door open for future researchers and writers to enter the dark house of pain to poke about just as she had done. Once inside, she had gained deeper knowledge of the slithering political realities that go largely unremarked by corporate journalism and unexamined in foundation-funded academic research.[24] Chang had stumbled across a venomous nest of vipers and was bitten hard, repeatedly. Though slowly poisoned, her core strength caused her to remain lucid amidst the institutionalized madness. Such fortitude allowed her to leave behind a wealth of written clues, personal leads, and questions that cry out for follow-up. Instead, the political importance of her legacy fades as Chang continues to be memorialized in books, statuary, and film by those no doubt motivated by the utmost sincerity. Let the example of Hemingway and his documented state-facilitated suicide serve as a reminder that repressive governments over the course of human history are the leading cause of death. If Iris Chang claimed that government forces were "hounding" her, then it would be wise to heed this last testament and treat it with the grave seriousness it warrants.

NOTES

[1] A. E. Hotchner, "Hemingway, Hounded by the Feds." *New York Times* 01 Jul. 2011. Http://www.nytimes.com/2011/07/02/opinion/02hotchner.html?pagewanted=all.

[2] Anthony Summers, *Official and Confidential: The Secret Life of J. Edgar Hoover* (New York: Pocket Star Books, 1994).

[3] M. Wesley Swearingen, *FBI Secrets: An Agent's Exposé* (Boston, Massachusetts: South End Press, 1995).

[4] Lydia Saad, "Americans: Kennedy Assassination a Conspiracy." Gallup 21 Nov. 2003. Http://www.gallup.com/poll/9751/americans-kennedy-assassination-conspiracy.aspx.

[5] Iris Chang, *The Rape of Nanking: The Forgotten Holocaust of World War II* (New York: Basic Books, 1997).

[6] Stephanie Losee, "The Demons You Know." *Salon.com* 13 Dec. 2007. Http://www.salon.com/mwt/feature/2007/12/13/paula_kamen.

[7] Paula Kamen, Finding Iris Chang: *Friendship, Ambition, and the Loss of an Extraordinary Mind* (New York: Da Capo Press, 2007).

[8] Ying-Ying Chang, *The Woman Who Could Not Forget: Iris Chang Before and Beyond the Rape of Nanking—A Memoir* (New York: Pegasus Books, 2011).

[9] John Marks, *The Search For the "Manchurian Candidate: The CIA and Mind Control* (New York: Times Books , 1979).

[10] Dominic Streatfeild, Brainwash: *The Secret History of Mind Control* (New York: St. Martin's Press, 2007).

[11] Peter R. Breggin, M.D., *Medication Madness: A Psychiatrist Exposes the Dangers of Mood-Altering Medications* (New York: St. Martin's Press, 2008).

[12] David Healy, *Let Them Eat Prozac: The Unhealthy Relationship Between the Pharmaceutical Industry and Depression* (New York and London: New York University Press, 2004).

[13] Kamen, 58.

[14] Frank Dikötter, *Mao's Great Famine: The History of China's Most Devastating Catastrophe, 1958-1962* (New York: Walker & Company, 2010).

[15] Bernard P. Wong, *The Chinese in Silicon Valley: Globalization, Social Networks, and Ethnic Identity* (Lanham, Maryland: Rowman & Littlefield Publishers, Inc., 2006).

[16] Rodham Watch, "Is the Other Hsu About To Drop? Hillary's Donor Linked to China Missile Trader." *WorldNetDaily* 02 Sep. 2007. Http://www.worldnetdaily.com/index.php?pageId=43335.

[17] Sterling Seagrave & Peggy Seagrave, *Gold Warriors: America's Secret Recovery of Yamashita's Gold* (London & New York: Verso, 2003).

[18] Iris Chang, *Thread of the Silkworm* (New York: Basic Books, 1995).

[19] Anthony Summers, *The Arrogance of Power: The Secret World of Richard Nixon* (2001), 164.

[20] Ed Rollins with Tom DeFrank, *Bare Knuckles and Back Rooms: My Life in American Politics* (New York: Broadway Books, 1996), 214.

[21] James S. Henry, *The Blood Bankers: Tales From the Global Underground Economy* (New York and London: Four Walls Eight Windows, 2003). Chapter Two, "Philippine Money Files" is particularly relevant, pp. 43-94.

[22] Colin A. Ross, M.D., *The C.I.A. Doctors: Human Rights Violations By American Psychiatrists* (Richardson, Texas: Manitou Communications, Inc., 2006).

[23] José Manuel Rodríguez Delgado, *Physical Control of the Mind: Toward a Psychocivilized Society* (New York: Harper & Row, 1969).

[24] Horace Freeland Judson, *The Great Betrayal: Fraud in Science* (Orlando, Florida: Harcourt, Inc., 2004).

DARRELL Y. HAMAMOTO is Professor of Asian American Studies at the University of California, Davis. The essay in this collection is part of a series concerning the dark side of contemporary Asian America within the New World Order. He has written a number of academic books and essays in media studies including *Nervous Laughter* (1989), *Monitored Peril* (1994), and *Countervisions* (2000). For the wider public, Hamamoto has produced films (*Yellocaust* [2004]), experimental music (*Voices* [1999]), and is currently working on a multi-media online performance piece titled *I Hate White People* based upon a verbatim diatribe by a former student. His interests include pre-1970s country music, boutique guitar amps, watching NHK World TV, abolishing the privately held Federal Reserve, and visiting habitable countries that might offer safe haven from societal decay and economic implosion in the US.

Interview with Ying-Ying Chang

by Larry Yu

The following interview with Ying-Ying Chang recounts her thoughts about the life, work, and tragic suicide of her daughter, Iris Chang, the renowned author of The Rape of Nanking *and other works. After Iris's suicide in 2004, Ying-Ying embarked on a journey of recollection and healing that culminated in her memoir about Iris,* The Woman Who Could Not Forget, *which has garnered significant public recognition since its publication in 2011. Ying-Ying's words bear eloquent testimony to a mother's love for her daughter and the passion that Iris embodied in both life and death.*

Larry Yu: Can you talk about the process of writing *The Woman Who Could Not Forget* and your thoughts in creating it?

Ying-Ying Chang: *The Woman Who Could Not Forget* is my memoir and also the biography of my daughter, Iris Chang. In 2004, when Iris died, I had already decided to write a memoir dedicated to her memory. I wanted people to know the true story of her life. The second reason: When Iris died, her son, Christopher, was only two years old, and he would never have been able to know his mother if I hadn't written a book about her life and work. Another reason is that there was much speculation about her death in the media that was not accurate. I wanted to set the record straight about her life.

Although I had written and published a number of scientific papers in my research career, I had never written or published a book before this one. English is my second language, and my Chinese is much better than my English. At the beginning, I could not decide whether to write the memoir in English or in Chinese.

After judging the vast number of letters and emails Iris wrote to us over the years, which I intended to include in the memoir, I decided it was far better to write and publish the book in English. I wanted to publish Iris's letters and emails in the original.

Originally, I was hoping to have a professional writer co-author the book, but I could not find one. I wrote the book without a ghost writer, and it took me almost 6 years. The first two years after Iris died, I was so sad I couldn't endure the pain of writing it. So, the first two years I devoted my time mainly to the activities of educating the younger generations (working with organizations such as Global Alliance for Preserving the History of World War II in Asia), but at the same time, I collected and categorized all the materials I could about her life and writing. From 2007 to 2009, I devoted one hundred percent of my time to writing the memoir. I did, however, hire a professional editor after I finished it. I'm very glad it worked out that way in the end.

I'm not a trained writer but a scientist, so I wrote the memoir and Iris's life in chronological order. As the writing progressed, I continued reading numerous letters and emails she had written to us—also her speeches. Her words inspired me very much and were the driving force that helped me complete the book.

LY: What was the most enjoyable aspect of writing or promoting your book? And what was the most difficult aspect of the book for you?

YC: The most enjoyable aspect of writing the book was describing her childhood and her reaching the goal of becoming a writer. Those lovely and joyful moments will never fade away in my memory. Of course, the most difficult moment was describing her death at the end. I devoted the last two chapters of the book to her death. Her breakdown and path to suicide occurred only in the last three months of her life. It's reassuring and relevant to keep in mind that in the 36 years of her short life, ninety-nine percent of that time was for Iris happy, exciting, and inspiring.

I traveled to a number of cities in North America in the past half year making speeches and signing books to promote my memoir. I was overwhelmed by the enthusiastic responses from audiences. Many people who came to my book events knew Iris Chang and her books and told me they admired and respected her. Those who did not know her told me that my book had given them a deep understanding of Iris—her inner thoughts, her compassion, conviction, and courage. It's been a very rewarding experience.

LY: What were the obstacles that Iris encountered in getting her book *The Rape of Nanking* published such as with *Newsweek* magazine in the U.S. and Kashiwashobo Press of Japan? And do you believe there was more political resistance from Japan or the United States in publishing *The Rape of Nanking* and raising popular awareness of the Nanking massacres in general?

YC: In chapters 13 and 15 of my book, I described the obstacles that Iris faced in getting the excerpt of her book *The Rape of Nanking* published in *Newsweek* and the Japanese translation of her book published by Kashiwashobo Press in Japan. In the case of *Newsweek*, the excerpt from her book was supposed to be published in the November 17, 1997 issue of the magazine, but it was delayed for two weeks. The delay was due to the fact that a number of Japanese companies pulled their advertisements from that issue of the magazine. The cancelation of Japanese advertisements from the magazine was the result of the right-wing forces in Japan wanting to keep Imperial Japan's massive war crimes hidden from the world and having the economic and political power to censor courageous writers like Iris. Essentially the same thing happened to the translation and publication of her book by Kashiwashobo Press. The Japanese right-wing groups exerted tremendous pressure on the publisher, including death threats, and succeeded in forcing Kashiwashobo Press to cancel the translation project. Finally, 10 years later, Iris's book was translated into Japanese and published in Japan.

Since the publication of the Nanking book, in spite of many excellent and positive reviews, there were still a few attacks. Iris felt that some academic "scholars" in Asian Studies programs in this country, particularly in Japanese Studies, might have been conspiring in a smear campaign to discredit her and her book—either out of jealousy or because their research funding came from Japanese sources. It's no secret that Japanese right-wing groups heavily finance the Japanese Studies and East Asian Studies programs in the U.S. and other countries. That financial support, however, generally has been disguised as research grants and awards. Consequently, publishing a book such as *The Rape of Nanking* could be very difficult for any academic institution whose funding comes mostly from Japan. Indeed, in his article "70 Years Later, Struggle for Nanking Massacre Justice Continues" in *The Atlantic* (May 26, 2011), Eamonn Fingleton stated, "Why the long silence in Western academies? Few East Asia specialists doubt what happened in the winter of 1937 to 38 ... . But the way that money flows in the East Asian studies field made such a book difficult to write. Nanking was, in a sense, a scholarly poisoned chalice. The East Asian field's funding comes overwhelmingly from corporations and foundations based in Japan and elsewhere in the region. Any scholar who broke the Nanking taboo would risk their funding."

LY: At the time of her death, Iris was working on a historical account of the Bataan Death March. Can you discuss the nature of this project and Iris's interest in this event?

YC: In 2004, Iris focused her research on a group of American World War II POWs in preparation for her next book. This was to be the story of the American 192nd Tank Battalion from the Midwestern states of Wisconsin, Illinois, Ohio, and Kentucky. The 192nd was deployed to the Philippines in 1941. They fought the Japanese and were subsequently captured by the Japanese Army. This tank battalion unit went through hell in the Philippines. There were some survivors, but many died from starvation, disease, and torture. In November 2003, Iris visited and interviewed several of the battalion survivors in those states. Later, she systematically interviewed and tape-recorded each one of them over the phone. This involved many hours of Q&A and was a long and tedious process. The stories of the surviving POWs were horrendous and excruciating beyond words. Iris said even her typist could not avoid weeping while she was transcribing the recorded tapes. This book project was certainly a dark subject and not good for her mental health, but Iris said she just could not turn her back on those veterans and let their stories be forgotten.

Right after the publication of *The Rape of Nanking*, we strongly suggested to Iris that she should not write about such a gruesome subject for her next book. At that point, she decided to write about the Chinese in America. As soon as we heard she was going to write the next book about the American POWs in the Philippines, we expressed our concern, but Iris said she could not forsake them.

LY: What lessons do you believe should be learned from Iris's tragic death, such as with respect to issues like the use of anti-depressant medication or mental health in the Asian American community?

YC: In the Epilogue of my book, I attempted to analyze Iris's death. I concluded that her suicide was triggered by the anti-depressants and anti-psychotic medications her doctors prescribed. Because I'm a biochemist, I did some investigation into the psychiatric drugs after she died. I was appalled to find out the serious potential side effects those drugs can have on mental patients. The most dangerous side effect is that patients can develop suicidal ideation and suicide preoccupation. I also found out that there are racial, ethnic, and gender differences in the response to psychiatric drugs. Asians seem to have a lower threshold for both the therapeutic and adverse effects of anti-psychotic drugs than Caucasians.

Mental illness is a taboo in many Asian cultures. Iris's death has brought up the topic of mental health in the Asian American communities. We need to discuss mental health issues openly. In this respect, my book and the death of Iris serve as a warning to Asian communities in this country. I hope people can learn from the lesson of Iris's tragic death and hopefully my book can save other people's lives.

LY: There has been speculation in some quarters about the circumstances of Iris's suicide. Darrell Hamamoto's "Double Suicide: The Deaths of Ernest Hemingway and Iris Chang Reconsidered" (included in this anthology) is one perspective on her death. Can you offer your general opinion of Hamamoto's essay and the insinuations he makes?

YC: I have read Professor Hamamoto's article, "Double Suicide: The Death of Ernest Hemingway and Iris Chang Reconsidered," and found the article very interesting and intriguing. Professor Hamamoto made an in-depth analysis of the death of both Ernest Hemingway and Iris Chang and concluded that both suicides might be the result of political persecution. The article has opened my eyes to such "Cold War mind control experiments" and "physical control of the mind," which I find very intriguing. In 2008, a point of view similar to Hamamoto's was published by *Counterpunch* in an article "A Final Injustice. Whatever Happened to Iris Chang?" written by Eamonn Fingleton (December 12, 2008). In the article, Fingleton wrote, "in the name of good U.S.-Japan relations, the State Department has long been even more fanatically hostile than the Japanese establishment in slapping down the Bataan survivors' quest for justice. In essence Chang was poking a stick in the eyes of two of the world's most powerful governments at once."

In the Epilogue of my book, I also expressed my thoughts on the circumstances surrounding Iris's death in the last six months of her life. There are certainly many questions in my mind as well as in many other people's minds (who have written to me) that at the present time we just cannot answer. We may never be able to answer those questions surrounding her death. We have to be aware that nowadays the technology of intelligence and espionage is so sophisticated that it could not generally be detected by the average person. Professor Hamamoto wrote in his article that "Chang mustered the courage to end her life by a method so disturbing and sensational that questions concerning the circumstances leading to this final act of resistance will be asked far into the future." There are certainly more questions than answers in the case of Iris Chang's suicide.

LY: What do you think should be the legacy of your daughter in terms of her life and work in general?

YC: The legacy of Iris Chang should be how she lived rather than how she died. People should remember what she accomplished in her life. Her book, *The Rape of Nanking*, exposed the forgotten holocaust of WWII, forever changing the way we view that terrible and tragic war in Asia. She was not only a writer and historian, but also a human rights activist. She "wanted to rescue those victims from oblivion, to give a voice to the voiceless." Iris inspired many, many people globally by her inner passion, dedication, and determination to preserve historical truth and to seek justice for the millions of victims. Iris was a woman whose heart beat passionately for those who suffered. She was a woman who would not, and could not, forget their agony, and she refused to let their stories go untold.

Iris believed in "The Power of One." She believed "One person can make an enormous difference in the world." She said, "One person—actually, one IDEA— can start a war, or end one, or subvert an entire power structure. One discovery can cure a disease or spawn new technology to benefit or annihilate the human race. You as ONE individual can change millions of lives. Think big. Do not limit your vision and do not EVER compromise your dreams or ideals." She followed her own advice, lived her convictions, and her work as a writer and historian has preserved the truth of history and awakened the conscience of the world.

Iris's life was short, but she left a legacy of a life full of courage and conviction, and a life's work that will continue to illuminate and inspire.

LARRY YU is the communications coordinator for the Thymos organization of Oregon. He is also a regular contributor to the Seattle-based *International Examiner* newspaper and has published work in *New America Media*, *Dissident Voice*, *Amerasia Journal*, *Journal of Asian American Studies*, and the API Movement blog. Larry teaches in the Ethnic Studies Department at Oregon State University and has a Ph.D. in English from Brown University. His interests include Asian American media, film, and radical politics.

YING-YING CHANG was born in China's wartime capital, Chungking, in 1940 and moved to Taiwan with her parents to escape from the Communists during the 1949 civil war. She grew up on the island and graduated from National Taiwan University in 1962. Ying-Ying came to the U.S. for graduate studies and received her Ph. D. in biological chemistry from Harvard University in 1967. She married Dr. Shau-Jin Chang, a Harvard physicist, in 1964.

In 1969, Ying-Ying and her husband started a teaching and research career spanning more than three decades at the University of Illinois, Champaign-Urbana. When they retired in 2002, they moved to San Jose, California.

After their daughter Iris Chang's untimely death in 2004, Ying-Ying and her husband channeled their energy into the preservation of the history of World War II in Asia. In the past several years, Ying-Ying and Shau-Jin have been invited by numerous groups and organizations in North America and China to speak and take part in activities related to their daughter's work and the Sino-Japanese war history.

Pacific Miles

by Victoria Yee

I.

Gripping tightly the airplane's arm rests,
Your tongue curls yet again over the strange words,
That jabs at your cheeks and pricks the flesh.
Mother's jewelry in the overhead compartment,
You clench tightly the paper with your brother's telephone
   number—
So tightly that blue ink runs over your fingers.

II.

Mother's eyes told you to leave,
and Father wouldn't even look at you.
The student Visa won't last, he said.
And neither will the money, she cried.
But you needed to get away from there.
And with that, you had to go anywhere.

III.

The smell of *ô-á-chian* zizzling,
And *wah ba sangs* hawking wares,
You forget, sometimes, they were yours.
Mother didn't recognize you,
When you came to her deathbed.
Who, and what, was foreign now?

VICTORIA YEE will graduate from Stanford University in 2013 with a B.A. in Asian American studies and a minor in Chinese. Her current interests include Asian American politics and psychology, East and Southeast Asian history, ethnic literature, rhetoric of mass mobilization and action, and of course, creative writing.

My Ramen Years
by Diem Tran

When my grandmother's hair started to fall out, my aunts bought her a White-lady wig, complete with curls attached to a pale, pink latex scalp. She seemed happy and would often wear it when company came to visit her.

Lying on the hospital bed a month later, she still had her wig on, but her own head looked as if it was too small for it. When she moved, the scalp with the White-lady cotton hair moved with her.

"Look, look, little ants crawling all over the sheet. How funny and small they are!" she pointed to nothing in particular.

The family gathered around, waiting for the moment to come. It didn't. Not on that day.

Two weeks later, we received a phone call that it was all over. I came to see her, resting on her own bed with her hands on her chest and the wig on the side of the bed.

Following this incident, our family became different. Perhaps it wasn't really the family, but more like each of us took on a new personality. My grandfather started to glorify Princess Diana and cut out a picture of her from a magazine, leaving her then husband, Prince Charles, behind. He framed it in a 4x6, and placed it next to Grandmother. The shrine on top of the TV was now completed, with pictures of these two women and statues of the Buddha and a Chinese man with a long beard wearing something that looked like a Goofy hat. They were surrounded by plastic fruits and incense sticks jutting out of an empty jasmine tea container.

On the day of the funeral, my mom was concerned that I didn't cry for the loss of my grandmother.

"Why aren't you sad? Don't you love her?" she asked, annoyed that she had brought up a cold and indifferent child.

"Of course I'm sad."

"She used to make cookies and put in more coconut for you than for the other kids."

"Yes, I know," I replied, lowering my eyes to look at my grandmother in the casket. She didn't look like Grandma from here. The aunts hadn't been satisfied with the makeup that the funeral artist had applied, so they had given her their own makeover with drugstore stuff. Now Grandma wore garish red lipstick and blue-teal eye shadow, ready to go to the next life as a hustler.

Of course, now wasn't the time to comment on this to my mother.

After the bowing, chanting, clanking of bowls by Buddhist monks, and a procession to the plot, we all went home.

Aunt #2 came over to talk to my parents. She was my mom's best sister, since her number was the nearest to my mom. They spent some time talking between themselves, occasionally looking my way.

On her way out, Aunt #2 came over to me and said, "Come, let's go shoe shopping."

She drove me to a small shoe store where they specialized in making shoes that smell like rubber. I didn't mind. It was better than going to the Salvation Army store where the only shoes I can ever find are either half a size too small or too large.

"Pick out any shoes you like!" she said, beaming.

Aunt #2 was special to me; at least that was what I was told. I called her Mom because according to my own mom, Mom #1, when I was born, a fortuneteller told her that I was going to be strong-headed and therefore would need two moms. So, Aunt #2 took on the task. She was happy to do it too, since she didn't have any kids of her own. I don't think she ever had to change my diapers or feed me, but just reaped the benefits of being called Mom.

"How about these?" I asked, shoving a pair of short, brown work boots into her hands.

She turned the boots over to admire the quality work and noted the proudly imprinted words, "Made in China."

"This is a boy's boots! Don't you want something pink and pretty?" She sounded just like my own mom who couldn't wait for me to wake up in the morning to pull my hair really tight into two ponytails and loop them around with two plastic flowers.

"These are neat. Look, they'll last forever!" I pointed to the bottom of the boots, tracing the masculine ridges of the rubber.

Aunt #2 is also a tightwad. She would never throw anything away. I once peeked inside her closet and saw an assortment of clothes that could belong in a period costume movie. My mom told me to be nice to her because one day, all of her stuff would be mine. I wasn't sure if that was a threat.

She counted her money carefully, looked at me as if she was conducting a huge favor and said, "Now, do you know how special you are to me?" Of course, she was only imploring me to thank her.

"Yes, I am very special. I truly don't deserve these shoes, Mom. Thank you so much for being kind."

That did it. She was touched. Her eyes gazed at me for a moment and she turned to look for the car, embarrassed that she was so moved.

"Come, let's have a talk," she said quietly, opening the car door on the passenger side. I slid in, carrying my new boots in a bag, cradling the box through the plastic.

"Do you miss Grandma?"

"Of course, I do," I replied, "But she has only been gone for a few hours or so."

She thought about my comment and then started to cry. Her tears started out silently but then they took on strength. She howled like an abandoned animal that had lost its pack. I felt bad for her and almost wanted to give her my new boots.

She finally turned to me. "Maybe you're too young now to understand how much love there is in your family. When I'm gone, I hope you'll remember me."

"Of course, I will remember you. You're my Mom #2, aren't you?"

She wiped her eyes and forced a smile, as if she knew that I was only half sincere. On the way home, she often turned to look at me and then at the bag in my hands.

My parents also began to change. Usually, they left my sister and me to fend for ourselves after school; we'd have a bag of chips and a can of grass jelly drink until they got home. Being a latch key kid wasn't too bad, especially when they reminded us of all the sacrifices they had made when we had left our country. My dad pushed his pride aside and tried to forget that he used to be a teacher, an inspector, and even a commander in the South Vietnamese army. Now, he stood behind a small lemonade stand on a golf course selling chips and soda to men in polo shirts and skinny women chucking Tab diet drinks. My mom, on the other hand, was tired but happy. She had found the secret ingredient to make all hamburgers taste better: MSG. She sprinkled a bit of this secret spice from a tin can on the frozen patty before she grilled them to perfection at the golf course café.

We were taught not to complain and to memorize the five tenets of being an immigrant:

1. Respect your parents.
2. Study hard, especially math.
3. Don't waste your time with extracurricular activities. Don't draw, do crafty projects, or sing in a choir. Playing a musical instrument is fine. Playing it well is even better, but don't waste too much time playing an instrument. Do math first.
4. The family is a unit, a living cell.
5. Someday, repay your parents.

My mom started to become more concerned that I was spending more time with my new boots than with her. It wasn't necessarily true, of course, but I wore them wherever I went, even when I was helping her peel shrimp and wash vegetables in the kitchen. Inside the apartment, I wore them wrapped with two plastic bags and anchored with rubber bands at the ankles so they wouldn't leave dirty marks on the matted brown carpet.

"You really like those boots, don't you?" she said, turning to stir the curry that was bubbling in the wok.

"Yes, I do."

"Your other mom is nice. It's a good thing she has more money than us. She was lucky she came over here earlier. It's always better to start a new life when you're younger ..." Her sentence trailed off, wistfully.

"But we're okay now, aren't we? We're not living off welfare anymore."

"Not after what happened at the rich people's store. That boy ... I knew I had to find any kind of job ... not be like those Cambodians." She motioned her head towards the neighbor's house. "Those people just keep making more kids so they can get a bigger welfare check. No shame at all."

Thanks to my mom, I now believe that all Cambodians eat with their hands and know how to screw the system.

She continued, "He called me 'ma'am' when I paid with food stamps! He looked down on us!"

"I don't think the word ma'am means a bad thing. It means that you're an older woman."

"Older woman? I've never been old. Well, it was your dad's fault for trying to take us on an outing to an all-White people's neighborhood. We're just too different and they looked down on us."

"Finished!" I interrupted eagerly, pointing to the pile of peeled shrimp. I stretched out my hands and went to the sink to wash.

She peered at the bowl and inspected the tails.

"Good, you got the tip of the tails out. Didn't waste them."

Done with the quality time spent with my mom, I went back to the corner of the apartment where I sat between our bed and an aluminum shelf that wobbled every time I pulled out a book. I took off my boots and placed them on the ledge of the window, making sure that they rested on top of the plastic bags. The brown fake leather was still shiny even after two months. Even though I'd kept the laces clean, the ends were starting to fray.

"Stop touching those boots all the time. Can't you play with your dolls or some other toys?"

She was truly amazing. Even from the kitchen, she knew what

I was doing.

True, I did have quite a few dolls, but every one of them had some kind of defect. My best doll had blue eyes that opened when I held her up, although on her Bad Eye Days, one would remain closed and I had to use my finger to pry it open. My other doll ... well, I had attempted to make her into the one I longed for, Baby Alive! She went through five minutes of intensive and laborious surgery with my dad's screwdriver and successfully came out with one hole in her mouth and another in her bottom. But unfortunately for that doll, she didn't digest rice very well. The kernels dried, and she had a problem with elimination. Now she made a piñata-like sound when I rocked her.

My sister, Anh, was the youngest in our family and a sensitive child. It was she who gave my parents their fear that I was cold and uncaring. On the day of the funeral, Anh started to cry when we approached the hearse. During the bowing and calling our name ceremony, her wailing became our background music. Her eyes, swollen from tears, forced the small epicanthal folds on her lids to be nonexistent for a day. She made the family proud.

"Look, Anh misses her grandma. Look at how much love and respect she has for her," said Aunt #4.

Aunt #5 stroked her hair. "She's crying for her sister." She turned to look at me accusingly.

My family monitored my emotional state for months to come, watching my reaction to their many attempts to expose me to sad and heartbreaking situations to see if they could trigger tears from me.

I was taken to a four-hour Chinese movie dubbed into Vietnamese. It was a beautiful love saga between a man, a woman, her ex-boyfriend, and the villagers. It was full of sad whiny ballads that would reach a cat-howling crescendo before suddenly plummeting into a bottomless abyss. To keep the male members of the audience awake, random flying Chinese warriors jumped out of trees when the ballads ended.

During one of the intermissions, Aunt #6 gazed at my face, checking for any signs of wetness. Unsatisfied but hungry, she went to get a few *banh mi* sandwiches and ice coffee at the concession stand.

My mom, a bit surprised by how much attention I'd been getting from her siblings, decided to partake in the game of Who Can Turn Her into an Emotional Girl? I'd never been wished, "Good night, don't let the bed bugs bite," probably because it would be too ironic given our past history of living in refugee camps. But now, instead of just "Good night," Mom would say "Grandma misses you." That always left me with a creepy feeling since it had been months since Grandma had died. I kept imagining how she would look now, her skin loose, if still existent under the polyester blouse with a large bow tie in the front. I hoped at least that the makeup had been rubbed off.

Every few weekends, Mom took the family to Grandma's grave, bringing along an Ouija board so we could speak to her spirit. Asking if she often thought of us, Grandma always answered, "Yes, I miss everyone, but mostly my best granddaughter, Thu." It was a long sentence to spell out, especially for a spirit who had to work with a plastic pointer made by the Hasbro people.

After chatting with Grandma, my dad took pictures of the family standing around the flowers on the plot. I made sure to leave some empty space next to me, just in case Grandma decided to join us for the family photo.

After mostly failed attempts to improve my behavior, the family dubbed me stoic and indifferent—a Black Sheep—one who was determined to amount to nothing. Most of my aunts and uncles became apathetic towards me, as if to show that they didn't want to waste their time on someone who would not cry at their funerals.

Only Aunt #2, successful with the shoes, decided not to give up on her pseudo daughter. She told my mom that perhaps I was confused from living in two cultures. Aunt #2 was happily married to an American man who provided them the comfortable La-Z-Boy lifestyle. Maybe, she said, my mom should Americanize me more quickly.

On Saturday mornings, my mom began serving me pizza for

breakfast, accompanied by a glass of milk mixed with lots of sugar and a few ice cubes. She had been inspired by my aunt as well as commercials featuring healthy, big-boned suburban kids who had fun parties orchestrated by a giant red chubby Kool-Aid guy.

One day, when Aunt #2 came over to check on us, my mom was in the middle of slicing up a hot dog and plopping them in my ramen bowl. "I do the best that I can, and God will take care of the rest," my mom said, embarrassed that she was feeding me packaged noodles which was not very Americanized at all.

I, in turn, looked at the bobbing chunks of pale, pink meat and became confused with what Mom had said to Aunt #2. God? Weren't we Buddhists? Now I had to re-explain that to my fifth-grade teacher who took a personal interest in the religion of each student in her class.

"What she needs is an American toy, like a Barbie doll!" Aunt #2 exclaimed.

Mom looked at her, thinking that I was fine with the doll collection from the bins at the thrift stores.

"Well, you just can't give up on her," Aunt #2 said, reading my mom's mind.

The summer weather of 1979 was rather unusual for southern California. It had rained repeatedly, wetting my grandmother's tomatoes and leaving the fragrant leaves to shrivel and droop like witch's fingers. I missed standing underneath the flimsy drain pipes and splashing in the many pot holes on my street in Saigon.

Bang, a lanky, milky-skinned Laotian girl who never thought of wearing shoes, became very curious about my boots. Whenever she had a chance, she would touch the brown man-made leather, tracing her fingers across the shoelace, hoping that I would let her try them on.

One day, she told me that my boots belonged to a boy.

"So, where is your brother, huh?" she asked, her tone lilted and mocking.

I wanted to push her down and smack her on that know-it-all face, but I held back. Who cared anyway; she wouldn't understand. I abruptly ended our game of hopscotch and swore to myself that I would never let her touch my boots again.

At home, I slammed the screen door, slid into a dejected squat before it, and poked my fingers into the small rips in the screen's netting. The holes, perfectly sized for my fingertips, welcomed in more flies.

I knew that if he were here, he would have defended me.

Anh, who had just turned six going on four, came over and stood next to me.

"I'm going to tell Mommy on you!" she pointed to the door.

I felt bad. It wasn't her fault that her older brother was never around for her. Little did she know that she was his stand-in. My parents never said that, of course, but I could tell from the way they treated her. My mother didn't bother to dress her in pink and allowed her pristine light skin to darken in the sun. I took her tanned hand and pulled her towards me. She sat in my lap, eyeing my boots.

"Do you want to try them on?" I asked, leaning to the side of her neck.

She turned to look at me, her eyes widening. I took the boots off and slipped them on her little feet. Anh became animated and squealed, flopping around the apartment with her sister's prized possession.

"They're warm!" she said, hopping from one foot to the other. "Are they always this warm?"

I answered with a simple, "Yes." But, what I really wanted to tell her was that "Yes, especially in the early morning after he had been wearing them around the house at night."

I didn't make this up. It was true. One night, I lay in bed, pretending to be asleep. About an hour after the street had become silent except for the occasional ambulance and movements from those working the late night shift near the dumpsters, I heard him, my brother.

I had left my boots, always clean, shined and ready for him on the same window ledge in case he decided to come. But earlier that day, I had lit two incense sticks instead of one, and snuck a Tootsie Pop lollipop next to the Buddha statue. More than anything, I just wanted to see what he looked like, how he had gotten on without our family, and if he was okay.

He came from nowhere, like all spirits usually do in the movies. He didn't tiptoe but just took small steps, being respectful of our sleep. I heard him because he had accidentally stepped on that spot on the carpet that had been splashed with a spill of Ovaltine from a week ago. His toes made a small crunch, just enough for me to know that he was in the room.

He went straight to the window ledge. He took down the boots and put them on, slowly, casually as if he had been doing this all his life. While tying the shoelaces, he turned towards our bed, checking to see if we were still asleep.

He stood in the boots, rocking back and forth like a child trying on shoes for the first time, took a few steps and glided above the carpet. From my one half-opened eye, I could see that he was walking over to us, his frame thin but tall, almost my height. I shut my eyes tight and, feeling him approach me, resisted the urge to sit up and pull him over. His hand wavered over my arm, hesitantly. Gently, he laid it down, his fingers slightly curved around my elbow. It was done very briefly, but at that moment, I realized that he was okay. He held it there for a few minutes and stared at my face. I didn't think I had breathed at all. He then walked over to my sister who was sprawled out on our bed. Her mouth opened, her face squished into the corner of her pillow. I wasn't too sure, but I think he smiled.

I couldn't share that story with my parents. They wouldn't believe me and I was afraid of bringing back the past, especially for my mom. Then I began to lose the details. His face became blurry, the features softened and faded with each passing day, leading me to believe that it had never happened at all.

I continued to light more incense sticks, stealing them when my mom wasn't looking and burning them in groups of threes or fours.

"Please, please come back," I pleaded, bunching the sticks in my hands and waving them in front of the altar, copying my mom's morning ritual. I stuck two lollipops and a bag of M&Ms to the side of Buddha as extra bribes.

Next time, I would not pretend. I would snatch and hold him tightly to me. I might even ask him if it was my fault that he couldn't be with us. "No," he would say to comfort me, "Mom wanted to search for your sandal on the bridge. She didn't want you to walk back to the hut barefooted. She had no idea that the bathroom bridge would collapse at that moment."

The throngs of people screaming while my father and I stand on the inland side of the bridge on that day still leave me weak. I often go back in my dreams, pulling my mom out before the stampede pushes her down, belly flat on the ground.

Of course I was to blame. If I had not been so careless and walked instead of skipped that day, the sandal would not have dropped somewhere on the bridge.

"Enough!" says my father in a firm voice, directing all of the hairs on my arms to stand and salute to the former commander. How long had he been standing behind me? Had he heard my mumbles? Perhaps he was only watching the trails of incense rising in curls and concerned that I was playing with fire. Or could it be that he finally realized that I had changed my grade in math by drawing a cunning line across the letter D to transform it into an honorable B?

Whatever his reason, he didn't reproach me. Since our time in Malaysia, he had trusted me to live according to my own heart, with him on the side to look on. During our months on that refugee island, every feeling on the face of the earth had been splayed out like the fish rationed to each family for their dinner. We didn't know what to do with them except to wallow and swallow.

He holds my boots that have been sunning on top of my window ledge. "These are meant for him, aren't they?"

It was the first time we had talked about my brother. Perhaps it was because we're Vietnamese or maybe it was just our genetic quirk, if you could call it that, but in our family, we ignore our problems rather than deal with them. Quit whining and complaining. Just accept—that was the way to solve all problems.

"Your father is wiser than he appears," he says with a smile, taking my silence as a reply and, squatting down next to me, folds his legs into the lotus position.

I wipe my eyes and sit on the stool, picking at the paint chipping off the end of one of the plastic legs.

"There, you see? You can cry. You have been saving your tears for him, that is all."

He leans over to hug me. I smell the scent of an old man who had navigated a lost boat full of people to an island and was now navigating his family to his New World.

"Did he have a name?" I ask, eager to talk.

"Yes, of course. But it would be better for you to accept if he remains nameless."

I stand up, feeling like a defiant child. He is wrong. I can never accept his death. Did they? Had they moved on, as if he had never existed? Should we not take a day out of the year to pay him respect? Can't you tell these things to me, Father, or will you just answer me with short Confucius-like proverbs, assuming that the vagueness of it all is wise?

My father looks down, rubs his legs and unwinds them. The way his head bows in this angle brings me back again to that day when he was with my mom, carrying her into a makeshift medical clinic on the island. His head was tucked into his chest, sullen, as if his soul had detached. So much for standing up to him; my courage drains.

He is done with what he had wanted to say and stands up as if he's forgotten something somewhere. Walking away, he leaves me there with the same heavy load.

I had taken the boots from him and put them on without tying the laces. The bottom has begun to wear away, leaving a small hole in the rubber, large enough to catch a little pebble. I leave the little rock in there, jagged and grey. It makes a noise when I take a step, reminding me that I am alive and he is not.

A year passes. We are all becoming Americans. My parents have been taking ESL classes at City College while learning a new skill called drafting. Within a year, they had jobs in a small company doing meticulous things with small specialized pencils and rulers on a tilted table. Within the same year, AutoCAD, a computer program, was released and took over the jobs of human drafters. It was too bad, because I think my mom rather enjoyed the international potlucks at her work. She was always beaming in the pictures, dressed in her purple embroidered *ao dai* gown with her arms wrapped around a plate of spring rolls.

But my parents' spirits have persevered. After all, they crossed many oceans, avoided pirates, and learned to be vegetarians on certain days out of respect for Buddha and the health of their colon. My father has found a teaching job where he gets to talk about the importance of isosceles triangles in one's life. My mom was hired as a sous-chef at a restaurant where she arranges vegetables and meat in perfect systematic angles on a plate and sprinkles a dash of MSG for luck when no one is looking.

Anh has become a first-grade bully, always sharpening her fangs on a kid's arm when she doesn't get her way. She told me it is much faster and more effective than using her words. Her days are usually spent as a hostage in the principal's office. When bailed, the aunt de jour who comes to pick her up will apologize to the principal and make an excuse that they are working on her problem at home, or that my parents are newly arrived immigrants, still wobbly from the boat. "You know, those poor Boat People," she would say, her eyes wide and her lips an exaggerated frown.

As for me, my principal thought I needed a tougher curriculum, so I am bussed each morning to a school where groups of sixth grade kids are divided into those who play Dungeon and Dragons and those who sneak lip-gloss in their preppy, rainbow backpack. I miss my Third World friends from my old school. Here, we all have to speak English and speak it well.

I do pretty well in most subjects, but I struggle to maintain my above average grades. Words often stare back at me without meaning; I stay up at night to search through pages of my English to Vietnamese dictionary or a set of encyclopedia that we bought from a grocery store. Between learning American history, remembering the order of the presidents who combined, were more complicated than the set of my aunts and uncles on both sides of my parents, and making lip gloss out of Vaseline and beet juice, I am really falling behind in my math class.

My brother has never come back, but I no longer expect his visit. He was done and has moved on. In our next life, hopefully as two humans and not as two worms, we will meet again. I take a shoelace from my boot, roll it up, and put it behind Buddha. Now my brother finally has a place in our family, and it is time for me to get back to my math.

Maybe it is natural that we each tweak our personalities to deal with changes. What choice do we have if we can't turn them away? I am sure that I was a distraction for my aunts and uncle to cope with the loss of their own mother and my mom decided to join the gang to amuse herself. But secretly, I think she coped by choosing to forget. As for me, well, that part was obvious.

DIEM TRAN is an aspiring writer who recently dabbled in the medical field. She resides in Pleasant Hill, California with her supportive and wonderful Serbo-Bosnian-Swedish husband and her six-year-old son who has a discerning taste in all things made out of chocolate and fish sauce (not together, of course). She hopes to write more meaningful and fun short stories in the near future.

On a side note, she also has a stash of ramen packages in her pantry, in many colorful flavors to remind her of the good old days.

Stories of Arrival: Youth Voices Project

Five young poets who appear in this special section of this anthology, Bikash Khada, Luan Nguyen, Mary Niang, Ngoc Minh Tran, and Souttalith Vongsamphanhn are students from Foster High School in Tukwila, WA. They participated in the Stories of Arrival: Youth Voices Project *under the direction of poet and teaching artist Merna Ann Hecht and Foster High School ELL teacher Carrie Stradley. The young people participating in this project have journeyed to Washington State from Afghanistan, Bhutan, Bosnia, Brazil, Burma, Burundi, Congo, Eritrea, El Salvador, Ethiopia, Haiti, India, Iraq, Kenya, Laos, Mexico, Nepal, Palau, Romania, Russia, Somalia, Sudan, Thailand, Tonga, Togo, Turkey, other parts of the U.S., and Vietnam. All are learning English. All have left behind members of their family on their journey here. Many of them will be the first in their families to graduate from high school and continue on to college.*

The students in this project, now in its fourth year, create poetry that tells of their life experiences leaving their countries and adjusting to a new country and culture. They share these poems with the larger community by recording their poems for broadcast on a local public radio station, and publishing an anthology of their work. Proceeds from the sale of the anthology, which includes a CD with each poet reading a poem, are donated to the Refugee Women's Alliance and to a college scholarship for a senior in the project who shows exceptional merit. The five poems that follow came from the 2010 anthology, Many Voices with One Heart: Voices of Global Youth *and the 2011 anthology,* The World is Our Heart, Poetry is Our Soul: Memories and Stories of Immigrant Youth.

The 2011 anthology is available for $20 (including mailing) and may be ordered directly through the project director by emailing mernaanna@yahoo.com.

My Dream
by Luan Nguyen

My dream is to be a workman in construction.
This dream follows me, since I was a child
playing with many bricks to make a house.
I want to build many beautiful and solid houses.
I dream of my future,
I could save some money,
to rebuild my old house in KonTum, Vietnam.
Because all of my childhood is in that house.
I don't want to lose it.

LUAN NGUYEN was born in 1990 in the city of Kon Tun in Vietnam. He lived in Kon Tun with his family for eighteen years. On January 21, 2008, Luan came to the U.S. with many beautiful dreams for the future. He hopes to be a construction worker and build many houses. Luan also wants to play sports. He dreams of saving money to return to Vietnam to visit his grandmother who loved and took care of him for eighteen years in Vietnam.

A Poem to My Eyes

by Souttalith Vongsamphanhn

Oh my eyes, why do you make me remember the thing I
saw?

It doesn't matter how far or how long ago it happened.
I still see it.

I have to leave my own home.
It is still in my dream.

Sometimes I try to forget the things that make me feel bad.
My land covered with blood.

But I cannot forget,
If I do that,
I would not belong to my people anymore,
I would not belong to my land anymore.

SOUTTALITH VONGSAMPHANHN was born in Laos.
He lived in Viangchan, the capitol city of Laos. He arrived
in Seattle to unite with his mother during the summer of
2007. Souttalith speaks three languages—Laotian, Thai
and English. He likes to break-dance and he hopes that
one day he will become a famous break-dancer.

Water Drum

by Bikash Khada

My life is like a water drum,
if it is full
then many people make me their relatives
by showing me love,
but, if the water drum is empty
then people cannot show me love.
If I am like an empty water barrel
then I am like curry without salt,
a monkey without a tail,
a country without peace,
a forest without trees,
coffee without sugar,
and human beings without their hearts.

BIKASH KHADA was born in Nepal. He is eighteen years old. For sixteen years, Bikash lived in a refugee camp with 20,000 people. He spent those years in a bamboo hut waiting for reparation, but it was not successful. His life in the refugee camp was very difficult in part because he could not get a quality education, though his family knew how education would be important in his life. Bikash had many dreams but his family couldn't afford them. The climate was intolerable and lacked medical facilities.  When Bikash finally left the refugee camp, he had to leave many of his near and dear loved ones forever. Fortunately, through IOM, he came to the USA on August 28, 2009. Now in the USA, Bikash has many dreams including becoming a dentist or doctor. He wants to be liked and trusted by all people so he can do good things for everyone. Bikash is proud of being Nepalese. He also dreams of helping both homeless and poor people.

What I Lived For??

by Mary Niang

I lived for stories about the war,
My father told me about my country, Chin State of Burma
It's like beehives falling from the trees, with angry bees.

I lived for listening to the sounds of my country
And I remember the sound of screaming,
From the villages when the soldiers came
The children were afraid with crying and
The sound from feet stomping through the village.

And I left my beautiful green land
Where the long river is flowing,
Where the long river, Meitei gun flows
And connects to India.

I lived to share the stories about my country
I lived because I want to know what is happening
in other countries.
Is the same thing happening in other countries, as in my
country?
Like a blustering wind that never calms down.

I lived for my strong heart to keep courage within myself
My feet are planted firmly on the rock.
The hard winds are blowing into all of my body,
It's like the wind wants to take my courage and all of me away,
It's like the rain and storm are starting and no one can stop
them,
It's like the weather never calms down, the rain keeps pouring,

Like my country fills itself with war and still
does not stop.

I lived so that someday I might see my motherland again,
When that day happens, the past and the present and all of the
pain
and the tears will rub into the face of my country,
My people will be happy again, like lost birds
who fly away from home and think never to find home again,
But these lost ones return, they are surprised, to find again
their home.

MARY NIANG was born in 1993. She is
seventeen years old. She will never forget New
Delhi and the way all Indian people celebrate
Republic Day which is a very big celebration.
Mary was born in Tungzang, Chin State of
Burma, close to India, Thailand and China. She
speaks and writes six languages—Tedim, Zo,
Teizang, Hindi, Mizo and English. Her goal is to become a doctor. She
also wants to travel all around the USA. Mary loves to write poetry and
make it into a song. She came to the USA on February 18, 2010. Before
coming to America, she lived in New Delhi, India. She grew up there
and did not have the chance to study because she didn't have enough
money. Now her dream of wanting to go to school is becoming real.
Mary is making a new life in the USA.

My Book of Memories
by Ngoc Minh Tran

My life is a library full of stories
My heart is a bookshelf
It stores my book of memories
My book has all of the happiness, sadness, love, and anger
My memory book is rich with my stories.

I remember the first time I cried when I was born
My mom's tears flow on my cheek,
My dad was screaming in a big voice
The "Welcome" word from the earth.

I remember the softness of the sand from the beach,
a taste of salt water from the sea
smell of ferns and their comfortable shadows.
I remember the difficult and miserable life of fishermen
And how hard a young boy had to work to get money.

I remember the time I ran more than I walked,
because I heard yelling more than talking
I remember the wish that I really wanted to be true.
I wished there would not ever be arguments in my family.
I wished we could sit down together and enjoy our family
dinnertime
something I never have, a peaceful family dinner,
even if it is just rice and fish sauce.

I remember I saw a boy who had his dad's love
I was running away with my heavy legs
Dad! I need you more than my candy box.

I remember how long I did not see my dad,
fourteen years, five months, without his love.
I can't wait until the day I can see him again,
Because even one day for me seemed like one century.

I remember when I came to the USA and saw my dad
like a bird finally found its own sky,
I remember the teaching from my dad
Everything you learn and you know
is only just one drop of water
from the large ocean.

I remember my fantastic dream.
I dreamt of being a bird, flying into the big sky,
I dreamt of being a snail, moving slowly with my life,
as I will leave my steps behind for the next generation.

And now, from my memory book I have only read chapter one
Flip the page, and how chapter two is ...

NGOC MINH TRAN was born in 1995. He is fifteen
years old. He was born in Phan Thiet, Vietnam, a beautiful
place with a beach and the hard life of a fisherman. His
fondest dream is that one day his family can live together
with no fighting or conflict, just enjoying a family dinner
as they never have before. Ngoc arrived in the USA on
August 19, 2009. He will never forget the day before he
left Vietnam when he held his mom as close as he could hold her. Ngoc
dreams of becoming a pilot, like being a bird, flying into the big sky.

The perspectives expressed in this anthology do not necessarily represent the views or policies of Thymos and others involved in the publication of this anthology.

Made in the USA
Lexington, KY
08 December 2012